High Protein Air Fryer Recipes Cookbook with Picture

101 Effortless Delicious and Healthy Meals Ideas for the Modern Cook

By Ava Mitchell

Copyright © 2023 by Ava Mitchell

No part of this publication, **"High Protein Air Fryer Recipes Cookbook with Picture,"** may be reproduced, stored in a retrieval system, or transmitted, in any form or by any means, including but not limited to electronic, mechanical, photocopying, recording, or otherwise, without the prior written permission of the publisher and author.

The publisher and author have made every effort to ensure that all the information in the book is accurate at the time of publication. However, the publisher and author make no representation or warranties concerning the accuracy or completeness of the contents of this book and expressly disclaim any implied warranties of merchantability or fitness for a particular purpose.

All the recipes, photographs, and other content included in this book are the intellectual property of the author, Ava Mitchell, and are protected by copyright and other intellectual property laws. Unauthorized use or duplication of this material without express and written permission from the author or owner is strictly prohibited.

Amazon KDP distributes Kindle and Paperback editions, and any disputes or claims relating to the book must be resolved according to the Amazon KDP terms and conditions. This publication is designed to provide general information regarding the subject matter covered. It is sold with the understanding that the author is not engaged in rendering legal, accounting, or other professional services. If legal advice or other expert assistance is required, the services of a competent professional person should be sought.

This book is a work of non-fiction. Any resemblance to actual persons, living or dead, or events is coincidental.

Introduction

Looking to put a healthier spin on your favorite meals without compromising taste or texture? Dive into the world of air frying with Ava Mitchell's latest cookbook, **"High Protein Air Fryer Recipes Cookbook with Picture"** This unique cookbook combines the allure of high-protein foods with the convenience and health benefits of the air fryer, redefining modern cooking.

Every recipe in this book is a testament to Ava's innovative culinary spirit, transforming simple ingredients into wholesome, high-protein meals that taste as amazing as they look. The book features stunning images that display the delicious final product and guide you through the process, ensuring your dishes are always perfect.

But Ava's work goes beyond just recipes. With every turn of the page, she provides inspirational ideas encouraging you to experiment and create your signature dishes. This book is more than a guide; it's an invitation to explore the boundaries of your culinary imagination, making it an indispensable companion for novice and seasoned cooks.

Available in both Kindle and Paperbag, " **High Protein Air Fryer Recipes Cookbook with Picture**" is more than a cookbook—it's your gateway to a healthier and tastier lifestyle.

Table of Contents

Chapter 1: High-Protein Poultry Dishes 8
Recipe 01: Air Fryer BBQ Chicken Breasts 8
Recipe 02: Garlic Herb Roasted Turkey Cutlets 10
Recipe 03: Air Fryer Chicken Parmesan 12
Recipe 04: Sesame-Ginger Chicken Thighs 14
Recipe 05: Buffalo Chicken Wings 16
Recipe 06: Healthy Turkey Meatballs 18
Recipe 07: Lemon-Pepper Chicken Drumsticks 20
Recipe 08: Healthy Chicken Nuggets 22
Recipe 09: Quinoa-Stuffed Chicken Breasts 24
Recipe 10: Maple-Dijon Glazed Chicken Thighs 26

Chapter 2: Flavorful Fish and Seafood 28
Recipe 11: Crispy Air Fryer Salmon 28
Recipe 12: Cajun Blackened Shrimp 30
Recipe 13: Lemon-Garlic Tilapia 32
Recipe 14: Air Fryer Calamari Rings 34
Recipe 15: Spicy Sriracha Tuna Steaks 36
Recipe 16: Healthy Fish and Chips 38
Recipe 17: Asian-Inspired Sesame Scallops 40
Recipe 18: Zesty Lemon Butter Cod 42
Recipe 19: Garlic Parmesan Shrimp 44
Recipe 20: Spicy Cajun Catfish 46

Chapter 3: Lean Meat and Pork 48
Recipe 21: Juicy Air Fryer Steak 48
Recipe 22: Herb-Crusted Pork Chops 50
Recipe 23: Healthy Air Fryer Meatloaf 52
Recipe 24: Rosemary-Garlic Lamb Chops 54
Recipe 25: Buffalo Bison Burgers 56
Recipe 26: Asian Glazed Pork Tenderloin 58

Recipe 27: BBQ Pulled Pork 60

Recipe 28: Air Fried Veal Scallopini 62

Recipe 29: Spicy Italian Sausage Links 64

Recipe 30: Healthy Turkey Bacon 66

Chapter 4: Plant-based Protein Dishes 68

Recipe 31: Crispy Tofu Nuggets 68

Recipe 32: Spicy Chickpea Patties 70

Recipe 33: Air Fryer Falafel 72

Recipe 34: Tempeh Bacon Bits 74

Recipe 35: Edamame and Quinoa Burgers 76

Recipe 36: Crispy Seitan 'Chicken' Tenders 78

Recipe 37: Sweet and Spicy Tofu Stir Fry 80

Recipe 38: Crunchy Lentil Fritters 82

Recipe 39: Air Fried Black Bean Taquitos 84

Recipe 40: BBQ Jackfruit Pulled Pork 86

Chapter 5: Protein-Packed Eggs & Dairy 88

Recipe 41: Air Fryer Omelette Cups 88

Recipe 42: Mozzarella Sticks 90

Recipe 43: Quiche Lorraine Bites 92

Recipe 44: Parmesan Crusted Hard-Boiled Eggs 94

Recipe 45: Air Fryer Frittata with Spinach and Feta 96

Recipe 46: Greek Yogurt Marinated Chicken 98

Recipe 47: Eggplant Parmesan Stacks 100

Recipe 48: Goat Cheese and Spinach Stuffed Chicken Breast 102

Recipe 49: Ricotta and Spinach Stuffed Shells 104

Recipe 50: Air Fried Halloumi Bites 106

Chapter 6: Nutritious Nuts and Seeds 108

Recipe 51: Air Fryer Roasted Almonds 108

Recipe 52: Air Fryer Spicy Cashews 110

Recipe 53: Garlic Parmesan Pumpkin Seeds 112

Recipe 54: Sweet and Spicy Pecans 114

Recipe 55: Chili Lime Pistachios 116

Recipe 56: Honey Roasted Sunflower Seeds 118

Recipe 57: Spiced Sesame Seed Mix 120

Recipe 58: Air Fried Walnuts with Rosemary 122

Recipe 59: Air Fryer Crunchy Peanut Butter Granola 124

Recipe 60: Cinnamon and Sugar Coated Almonds 126

Chapter 7: Protein Snacks and Starters 128

Recipe 61: Air Fryer Cheese and Bacon Rolls 128

Recipe 62: Crunchy Zucchini Fries 130

Recipe 63: Air Fryer Protein Packed Quesadilla 132

Recipe 64: Jalapeno Poppers with Cream Cheese and Bacon 134

Recipe 65: Buffalo Cauliflower Bites 136

Recipe 66: Cheesy Spinach and Artichoke Dip 138

Recipe 67: Air Fryer Mini Sliders 140

Recipe 68: Chicken Satay Skewers with Peanut Sauce 142

Recipe 69: Spiced Chickpea Popcorn 144

Recipe 70: Cheesy Pepperoni Protein Pizza Rolls 146

Chapter 8: Power Breakfast Recipes 148

Recipe 71: Protein-Packed French Toast Sticks 148

Recipe 72: Ham and Egg Breakfast Burritos 150

Recipe 73: Breakfast Sausage Links 152

Recipe 74: Bacon and Cheese Muffins 154

Recipe 75: Spinach and Feta Egg White Wraps 156

Recipe 76: Turkey Sausage Patties 158

Recipe 77: Sweet Potato and Black Bean Breakfast Burritos 160

Recipe 78: Greek Yogurt Pancakes 162

Recipe 79: Bacon, Egg, and Cheese Biscuits 164

Recipe 80: Protein Power Smoothie Bowl 166

Chapter 9: High Protein Desserts 168

Recipe 81: Air Fryer Protein Brownies 168

Recipe 82: Protein-Packed Apple Fritters 170

Recipe 83: Banana Nut Protein Muffins 172

Recipe 84: Greek Yogurt Cheesecake Bites 174

Recipe 85: Almond Joy Protein Balls 176

Recipe 86: Pumpkin Protein Donuts 178

Recipe 87: High Protein Lemon Bars 180

Recipe 88: Peanut Butter Protein Cookies 182

Recipe 89: Strawberry Protein Crepes 184

Recipe 90: Chocolate Chip Protein Scones 186

Chapter 10: Full Meal Preps 188

Recipe 91: Air Fryer BBQ Chicken with Quinoa and Broccoli 188

Recipe 92: Mediterranean Salmon with Couscous and Asparagus 190

Recipe 93: Beef and Broccoli Stir Fry 192

Recipe 94: Grilled Turkey with Sweet Potatoes and Brussels Sprouts 194

Recipe 95: Lemon Garlic Shrimp with Zucchini Noodles 196

Recipe 96: Asian Inspired Chicken and Vegetable Stir Fry 198

Recipe 97: Pork Tenderloin with Sweet Potatoes and Green Beans 200

Recipe 98: Cajun Catfish with Rice and Okra 202

Recipe 99: Stuffed Bell Peppers with Ground Turkey and Brown Rice ...204

Recipe 100: Spicy Sausage and Vegetable Skillet 206

Recipe 101: Easter Lamb with Rosemary and Garlic 208

Conclusion 210

Chapter 1: High-Protein Poultry Dishes

Recipe 01: Air Fryer BBQ Chicken Breasts

Savor the succulence of barbecue without stepping outside with this simple yet flavorful Air Fryer BBQ Chicken Breasts recipe. It's a perfect smokey, sweet, and juicy blend - a game-changer for weekday dinners!

Servings: 4

Prepping Time: 10 minutes

Cook Time: 20 minutes

Difficulty: Easy

Ingredients

- ✓ 4 boneless, skinless chicken breasts
- ✓ 1 cup of your favorite barbecue sauce
- ✓ Salt and pepper to taste
- ✓ 1 tablespoon olive oil

Step-by-Step Preparation

1. Pat the chicken dry and season both sides with salt and pepper.
2. Preheat the air fryer to 375°F (190°C).
3. Lightly brush the chicken breasts with olive oil.
4. Place the chicken in the air fryer and cook for 10 minutes.
5. Flip the chicken, generously brush it with barbecue sauce, then cook for another 10 minutes or until the internal temperature reaches 165°F (74°C).
6. Let the chicken rest for a few minutes before serving.

Nutritional Facts: (Per Serving)

- Calories: 285
- Total Fat: 6g
- Saturated Fat: 1.5g
- Cholesterol: 85mg
- Sodium: 690mg
- Total Carbohydrate: 18g
- Dietary Fiber: 0g
- Sugars: 16g
- Protein: 36g

Enjoy this tender, juicy BBQ chicken perfectly cooked in your air fryer. This easy recipe will have you looking forward to mealtime, as it packs all the barbecue flavor without the hassle. Perfect with a side of fresh salad or roasted veggies.

Recipe 02: Garlic Herb Roasted Turkey Cutlets

Elevate your meal times with Air Fryer Garlic Herb Roasted Turkey Cutlets - a dish oozing with flavor and tenderness. Perfect for a midweek dinner yet unique enough for guests, these cutlets are your ticket to a healthy, mouthwatering meal.

Servings: 4

Prepping Time: 10 minutes

Cook Time: 15 minutes

Difficulty: Easy

Ingredients:

- 4 turkey cutlets
- 3 cloves garlic, minced
- 2 tablespoons olive oil
- 1 tablespoon fresh rosemary, finely chopped
- 1 tablespoon fresh thyme, finely chopped
- Salt and pepper to taste

Step-by-Step Preparation:

1. Mix minced garlic, olive oil, rosemary, thyme, salt, and pepper in a bowl.
2. Brush this mixture evenly on both sides of the turkey cutlets.
3. Preheat the air fryer to 375°F.
4. Arrange the cutlets in the air fryer basket, ensuring they do not overlap.
5. Cook for 15 minutes or until the internal temperature reaches 165°F, flipping once halfway through.
6. Let the cutlets rest for a few minutes before serving.

Nutritional Facts: (Per Serving)

- Calories: 240 kcal
- Total Fat: 10g
- Saturated Fat: 2g
- Cholesterol: 75mg
- Total Carbohydrates: 1g
- Protein: 34g
- Sodium: 75mg
- Fiber: 0g
- Sugar: 0g

Air Fryer Garlic Herb Roasted Turkey Cutlets are a marvelous way to savor a lean protein most deliciously. This dish promises succulence and an exquisite blend of flavors, and with the convenience of an air fryer, you'll love how effortlessly this gourmet meal comes together. Enjoy the essence of good eating!

Recipe 03: Air Fryer Chicken Parmesan

Delight your family with this savory Air Fryer Chicken Parmesan. It is a quick and healthy spin on the traditional Italian classic with a satisfying crunch on the outside and juicy chicken within.

Servings: 4

Prepping Time: 10 minutes

Cook Time: 20 minutes

Difficulty: Easy

Ingredients

- ✓ 4 boneless chicken breasts
- ✓ 1 cup panko breadcrumbs
- ✓ 1/2 cup Parmesan cheese, grated
- ✓ 1/2 cup mozzarella cheese, shredded
- ✓ 1 cup marinara sauce
- ✓ 1 tsp garlic powder

- ✓ Salt and pepper to taste
- ✓ Cooking spray

Step-by-Step Preparation

1. Preheat the air fryer to 375°F.
2. Season the chicken breasts with salt, pepper, and garlic powder.
3. Mix the panko breadcrumbs and Parmesan cheese, then coat the chicken.
4. Cook in the air fryer for 10 minutes.
5. Mix marinara sauce and mozzarella cheese and cook for another 10 minutes until golden and bubbly.

Nutritional Facts: (Per Serving)

- ❖ Calories: 350
- ❖ Fat: 10g
- ❖ Carbohydrates: 15g
- ❖ Protein: 45g
- ❖ Sodium: 700mg
- ❖ Fiber: 2g

In under 30 minutes, you have a tasty and healthier Air Fryer Chicken Parmesan, delivering delightful crunch and flavor. This dish brings a slice of Italy to your dinner table with minimum effort and maximum satisfaction.

Recipe 04: Sesame-Ginger Chicken Thighs

Add an Asian twist to your chicken dinner with these Air Fryer Sesame-Ginger Chicken Thighs. Succulent and bursting with flavor, they make a perfect weeknight meal. Each bite is a delightful mix of sesame and ginger, making your dining experience extraordinary.

Servings: 4

Prepping Time: 10 minutes

Cook Time: 20 minutes

Difficulty: Easy

Ingredients:

- ✓ 4 bone-in, skin-on chicken thighs
- ✓ 2 tablespoons sesame oil
- ✓ 3 tablespoons soy sauce
- ✓ 1 tablespoon fresh ginger, grated
- ✓ 2 cloves garlic, minced
- ✓ 1 tablespoon sesame seeds

- ✓ Salt and pepper to taste
- ✓ Fresh scallions for garnish

Step-by-Step Preparation:

1. Mix sesame oil, soy sauce, ginger, garlic, sesame seeds, salt, and pepper in a bowl.
2. Marinate chicken thighs in the mixture for at least 30 minutes.
3. Preheat the air fryer to 180°C (350°F) for 5 minutes.
4. Arrange chicken thighs in the air fryer basket, skin side down.
5. Cook for 10 minutes, flip, and cook for another 10 minutes until golden and crispy.
6. Garnish with fresh scallions and serve.

Nutritional Facts: (Per Serving)

- ❖ Calories: 350
- ❖ Fat: 22g
- ❖ Protein: 28g
- ❖ Carbs: 4g
- ❖ Fiber: 1g
- ❖ Sugar: 1g

These Air Fryer Sesame-Ginger Chicken Thighs are more than just a simple meal; they're an adventure in flavor. Easy to prepare yet impressive, they will be a hit with the whole family. Serve with a side of steamed veggies or rice, and enjoy the delightful Asian taste that dances on your palate.

Recipe 05: Buffalo Chicken Wings

Savor the delight of crispy buffalo chicken wings with less guilt. This recipe uses an air fryer to get that perfect crunch without deep frying. Air fryer buffalo chicken wings are a crowd-pleaser and a must-try for any wing lover.

Servings: 4

Prepping Time: 10 minutes

Cook Time: 25 minutes

Difficulty: Easy

Ingredients:

- 2 lbs chicken wings
- 1 cup buffalo wing sauce
- 1 tablespoon olive oil
- Salt and pepper to taste
- Celery sticks and blue cheese dressing for serving

Step-by-Step Preparation:

1. Preheat your air fryer to 375°F.
2. Toss the chicken wings with olive oil, salt, and pepper.
3. Place the wings in the air fryer basket and cook for 25 minutes or until crispy and fully cooked, shaking halfway through.
4. Toss the cooked wings with buffalo sauce until thoroughly coated in a large bowl.
5. Serve hot with celery sticks and blue cheese dressing.

Nutritional Facts: (Per Serving)

- Calories: 410
- Fat: 28g
- Protein: 35g
- Carbs: 1g
- Cholesterol: 85mg
- Sodium: 1700mg

These Air Fryer Buffalo Chicken Wings are a sure hit for game nights, get-togethers, or family dinners. Using the air fryer, you get all the flavors and textures of traditional wings without the added calories from deep frying. Happy cooking!

Recipe 06: Healthy Turkey Meatballs

Jump-start your healthy eating habits with these mouthwatering Air Fryer Healthy Turkey Meatballs. These protein-rich balls are juicy, flavorful, and perfect as an appetizer or main course. You'll fall in love with the perfect blend of spices that highlight the natural taste of turkey.

Servings: 4

Prepping Time: 15 minutes

Cook Time: 15 minutes

Difficulty: Easy

Ingredients:

- 1 lb ground turkey
- 1/2 cup whole wheat breadcrumbs
- 1/4 cup grated Parmesan cheese
- 1/4 cup chopped fresh parsley
- 2 cloves garlic, minced
- 1 egg, beaten

- ✓ Salt and pepper to taste
- ✓ Cooking spray

Step-by-Step Preparation:

1. Combine ground turkey, breadcrumbs, Parmesan, parsley, garlic, egg, salt, and pepper in a large bowl. Mix until well combined.
2. Form into small meatballs, about 1 inch in diameter.
3. Preheat the air fryer to 400°F (200°C). Lightly spray the basket with cooking spray.
4. Arrange meatballs in a single layer in the air fryer basket. Cook for 15 minutes or until cooked through and browned on the outside, turning halfway through.

Nutritional Facts: (Per serving)

- ❖ Calories: 270 kcal
- ❖ Fat: 13g
- ❖ Protein: 30g
- ❖ Carbs: 10g
- ❖ Fiber: 1g
- ❖ Sugar: 1g

These Air Fryer Healthy Turkey, Meatballs, are a hit in any setting, offering a nutritious and delightful experience. This quick and easy recipe proves that eating healthy doesn't compromise taste. Packed with protein and flavor, they're a guilt-free treat you can enjoy anytime!

Recipe 07: Lemon-Pepper Chicken Drumsticks

Experience a flavor explosion with these Lemon-Pepper Chicken Drumsticks. A perfect blend of tangy, spicy, and savory, this recipe is ideal for a family dinner or weekend cookout. Enjoy the mouthwatering drumsticks that are crispy on the outside and juicy on the inside.

Servings: 4

Prepping Time: 15 Minutes

Cook Time: 40 Minutes

Difficulty: Easy

Ingredients:

- ✓ 8 chicken drumsticks
- ✓ 2 lemons (zest and juice)
- ✓ 2 tablespoons black pepper
- ✓ 1 tablespoon olive oil
- ✓ 2 garlic cloves, minced
- ✓ Salt to taste

Step-by-Step Preparation:

1. Preheat your air fryer to 425°F (220°C).
2. Combine lemon zest, juice, minced garlic, black pepper, olive oil, and salt in a bowl.
3. Toss the drumsticks in the mixture until well-coated.
4. Arrange the drumsticks on a baking tray lined with baking paper.
5. Bake for 40 minutes, flipping halfway through, until golden and fully cooked.

Nutritional Facts: (Per serving)

- Calories: 271 kcal
- Fat: 16g
- Protein: 27.1g
- Carbohydrates: 3.2g
- Sodium: 104.2mg
- Cholesterol: 139.5mg

With just a few ingredients, these Lemon-Pepper Chicken Drumsticks are super easy to prepare and utterly delicious. Enjoy them hot off the oven with fresh salad or roasted veggies for a complete meal. They're guaranteed to be a hit at your next gathering!

Recipe 08: Healthy Chicken Nuggets

In this recipe, we will create delicious Air Fryer Healthy Chicken Nuggets. These nuggets are crispy, golden brown, perfect for a healthy snack or meal, and prepared with fewer fats and oils than traditional methods.

Servings: 4

Prepping Time: 20 minutes

Cook Time: 15 minutes

Difficulty: Easy

Ingredients:

- ✓ 2 boneless, skinless chicken breasts
- ✓ 1 cup panko breadcrumbs
- ✓ 1/2 cup all-purpose flour
- ✓ 1/2 teaspoon salt
- ✓ 1/4 teaspoon black pepper
- ✓ 2 large eggs

- ✓ 1/2 teaspoon paprika
- ✓ Non-stick cooking spray

Step-by-Step Preparation:

1. Cut chicken breasts into bite-sized pieces.
2. Season the chicken with salt, pepper, and paprika.
3. Dredge the chicken pieces in flour, dip them in beaten eggs, then coat them with panko breadcrumbs.
4. Preheat the air fryer to 200°C (390°F).
5. Arrange the nuggets in the air fryer basket, ensuring they do not overlap.
6. Spray the nuggets lightly with cooking spray.
7. Cook for 15 minutes, flipping halfway, until golden brown and fully cooked.

Nutritional Facts: (Per serving)

- ❖ Calories: 210
- ❖ Protein: 22g
- ❖ Carbohydrates: 16g
- ❖ Fat: 5g
- ❖ Sodium: 340mg

Savor these Air Fryer Healthy Chicken Nuggets with your favorite dipping sauce for an indulgent yet healthier treat. Not only are these nuggets delightfully tasty, but their preparation also ensures a reduction in excess oils. Perfect for families and children, they are a delicious way to enjoy a comfort food favorite in a more health-conscious manner.

Recipe 09: Quinoa-Stuffed Chicken Breasts

Elevate your weeknight dinner with this healthy and delightful Air Fryer Quinoa-Stuffed Chicken Breasts recipe. This dish promises a mouthful of flavors while being guilt-free.

Servings: 4

Prepping Time: 20 minutes

Cook Time: 20 minutes

Difficulty: Easy

Ingredients:

- ✓ 4 boneless, skinless chicken breasts
- ✓ 1 cup cooked quinoa
- ✓ 1/2 cup diced bell peppers
- ✓ 1/2 cup diced onions
- ✓ 1/2 cup chopped spinach
- ✓ 1 clove garlic, minced

- ✓ 1 teaspoon salt
- ✓ 1/2 teaspoon black pepper
- ✓ 2 tablespoons olive oil
- ✓ 1 tablespoon paprika

Step-by-Step Preparation:

1. Preheat the air fryer to 180°C (360°F).
2. Butterfly the chicken breasts, being careful not to cut all the way through.
3. Mix a bowl of quinoa, bell peppers, onions, spinach, garlic, salt, and pepper.
4. Stuff the chicken breasts with the quinoa mixture and secure them with toothpicks.
5. Rub the chicken with olive oil and sprinkle with paprika.
6. Place the chicken in the air fryer basket and cook for 20 minutes or until the chicken is fully cooked.
7. Allow to cool before serving.

Nutritional Facts: (Per serving)

- ❖ Calories: 300
- ❖ Protein: 28g
- ❖ Fat: 9g
- ❖ Carbs: 24g
- ❖ Fiber: 3g
- ❖ Sugar: 2g

This Air Fryer Quinoa-Stuffed Chicken Breasts recipe creates a symphony of flavors with every bite while keeping your health in check. It's an easy-to-make, delicious dish that would win everyone's heart at the dining table. Enjoy the perfect harmony of nutrition and taste today!

Recipe 10: Maple-Dijon Glazed Chicken Thighs

Gather around for an exquisite dinner with this air fryer maple-Dijon glazed chicken thighs. The succulent chicken enveloped in a sweet, tangy glaze makes a perfect quick meal. Impress your loved ones with this restaurant-quality dish prepared right in your kitchen.

Servings: 4

Prepping Time: 10 minutes

Cook Time: 25 minutes

Difficulty: Easy

Ingredients:

- ✓ 4 chicken thighs, skin-on, bone-in
- ✓ Salt and pepper to taste
- ✓ 1/4 cup Dijon mustard
- ✓ 1/4 cup maple syrup
- ✓ 2 garlic cloves, minced

- ✓ 1 tablespoon olive oil
- ✓ 1 tablespoon fresh rosemary, chopped

Step-by-Step Preparation:

1. Preheat the air fryer to 380°F (193°C).
2. Season chicken thighs with salt and pepper.
3. Mix Dijon mustard, maple syrup, minced garlic, and olive oil in a bowl.
4. Coat the chicken evenly with the mustard-maple mixture.
5. Place chicken thighs in the air fryer basket and cook for 20-25 minutes until golden brown and cooked through, turning once.
6. Sprinkle with fresh rosemary before serving.

Nutritional Facts: (Per serving)

- ❖ Calories: 420 kcal
- ❖ Protein: 32g
- ❖ Fat: 25g
- ❖ Carbohydrates: 20g
- ❖ Fiber: 0.5g
- ❖ Sugar: 17g
- ❖ Sodium: 600mg

These delicious Air Fryer Maple-Dijon Glazed Chicken Thighs blend sweetness and tanginess, making them a delightful main course for any occasion. Enjoy the incredible convenience of an air fryer meal without sacrificing the taste and quality. Your family will be requesting this dish again soon!

Chapter 2: Flavorful Fish and Seafood

Recipe 11: Crispy Air Fryer Salmon

Enjoy a healthy yet deliciously crispy air fryer salmon, perfect for those following a low-carb diet. This salmon recipe is bursting with flavors from the honey garlic glaze and is sure to become a staple in your weekly menu.

Servings: 4

Prepping Time: 10 minutes

Cook Time: 12 minutes

Difficulty: Easy

Ingredients:

- ✓ 4 Salmon fillets
- ✓ Salt and pepper, to taste
- ✓ 2 tbsp Olive oil
- ✓ 2 cloves garlic, minced

- ✓ 3 tbsp Honey
- ✓ 2 tbsp Soy sauce
- ✓ 1 tbsp Lemon juice
- ✓ Fresh dill for garnish

Step-by-Step Preparation:

1. Preheat your air fryer to 400°F (200°C).
2. Season each salmon fillet with salt and pepper.
3. Mix the olive oil, minced garlic, honey, soy sauce, and lemon juice in a bowl to create a glaze.
4. Brush the glaze over the salmon fillets.
5. Place the salmon fillets in the air fryer and cook for 12 minutes or until the salmon is crispy and cooked.
6. Garnish with fresh dill and serve.

Nutritional Facts: (Per serving)

- ❖ Calories: 365
- ❖ Fat: 20g
- ❖ Protein: 34g
- ❖ Carbohydrates: 14g
- ❖ Fiber: 0g
- ❖ Sugar: 12g

This crispy air fryer salmon is not just easy and quick to prepare, but it's also a healthy and flavorful meal option. The combination of a sweet and savory glaze with the crispiness from the air fryer makes this dish a crowd-pleaser. Serve it with a fresh salad or your favorite side for a complete meal.

Recipe 12: Cajun Blackened Shrimp

Experience the rich, spicy notes of the bayou with this Air Fryer Cajun Blackened Shrimp recipe. Quick, easy, and healthful, it's the perfect weekday meal or party appetizer.

Servings: 4

Prepping Time: 10 minutes

Cook Time: 10 minutes

Difficulty: Easy

Ingredients:

- ✓ 1 lb large shrimp, peeled and deveined
- ✓ 2 tablespoons olive oil
- ✓ 1 tablespoon Cajun seasoning
- ✓ 1/2 teaspoon garlic powder
- ✓ Fresh parsley for garnish
- ✓ Lemon wedges for serving

Step-by-Step Preparation:

1. Mix the shrimp, olive oil, Cajun seasoning, and garlic powder until well coated.
2. Preheat your air fryer to 400°F (200°C).
3. Arrange the shrimp in a single layer in the air fryer basket.
4. Cook for 5-7 minutes or until the shrimp are pink and cooked.
5. Garnish with fresh parsley and serve with lemon wedges.

Nutritional Facts: (Per serving)

- Calories: 158
- Total Fat: 6.9g
- Saturated Fat: 1.1g
- Cholesterol: 172mg
- Sodium: 884mg
- Carbohydrates: 2.3g
- Fiber: 0.5g
- Sugar: 0.2g
- Protein: 21.6g.

This Air Fryer Cajun Blackened Shrimp offers a mouthwatering blend of spice and succulence, transporting your tastebuds straight to Louisiana. Quick to make and packed with flavor, it's an impressive dish that never disappoints.

Recipe 13: Lemon-Garlic Tilapia

This scrumptious Air Fryer Lemon-Garlic Tilapia will impress everyone at the dinner table. Its light, flaky texture, tangy citrus kick, and hint of garlic create a healthy, flavorful fish dish. An excellent choice for quick weekday dinners or fancy gatherings.

Servings: 4

Prepping Time: 10 minutes

Cook Time: 10 minutes

Difficulty: Easy

Ingredients:

- ✓ 4 Tilapia fillets
- ✓ 2 lemons
- ✓ 4 cloves garlic, minced
- ✓ Salt and pepper to taste
- ✓ 2 tablespoons olive oil
- ✓ Fresh parsley for garnish

Step-by-Step Preparation:

1. Preheat your air fryer to 400°F.
2. Pat dry the tilapia fillets. Drizzle with olive oil, and season with salt, pepper, minced garlic, and lemon zest. Squeeze half a lemon's juice over each fillet.
3. Place the fillets in the air fryer basket. Cook for 10 minutes until the fish is flaky and cooked through.
4. Garnish with fresh parsley and serve with lemon slices on the side.

Nutritional Facts: (Per serving)

- **Calories: 200 kcal**
- **Protein: 34g**
- **Fat: 6g**
- **Carbs: 4g**
- **Cholesterol: 85g**
- **Dietary Fiber:**

With minimal prep time, this Air Fryer Lemon-Garlic Tilapia is the perfect blend of ease and elegance. A delightful way to include healthy protein in your meals, this dish is sure to become a household favorite. Pair it with steamed veggies or a light salad for a well-rounded meal.

Recipe 14: Air Fryer Calamari Rings

Add a Mediterranean flair to your dinner with Air Fryer Calamari Rings. These delightfully crispy, golden rings are a lighter take on the deep-fried classic. Ideal as an appetizer or main course, they're sure to impress your guests.

Servings: 4

Prepping Time: 15 minutes

Cook Time: 10 minutes

Difficulty: Intermediate

Ingredients:

- 1 lb fresh calamari rings
- 1 cup flour
- 2 eggs, beaten
- 1 cup breadcrumbs
- 1/2 tsp salt
- 1/2 tsp black pepper

- ✓ 1/2 tsp garlic powder
- ✓ 1/2 tsp paprika
- ✓ Cooking spray
- ✓ Lemon wedges and marinara sauce for serving

Step-by-Step Preparation:

1. Preheat the air fryer to 400°F.
2. Combine flour, salt, pepper, garlic powder, and paprika in a shallow bowl.
3. Dip each calamari ring into the flour mixture, then into the beaten eggs, and finally, coat with breadcrumbs.
4. Arrange the coated calamari rings in the air fryer basket. Spray with a bit of cooking spray.
5. Cook for 10 minutes until golden brown and crispy, turning halfway through.
6. Serve with lemon wedges and marinara sauce.

Nutritional Facts: (per serving)

- ❖ Calories: 276
- ❖ Protein: 23g
- ❖ Carbs: 34g
- ❖ Fat: 5g
- ❖ Fiber: 2g
- ❖ Sugar: 2g

Discover the healthier side of your favorite seafood treats with Air Fryer Calamari Rings. This dish is a testament to how simple ingredients can make something incredibly delicious. It's the perfect way to bring restaurant-quality calamari into the comfort of your own home.

Recipe 15: Spicy Sriracha Tuna Steaks

Experience a flavorful journey with these Air Fryer Spicy Sriracha Tuna Steaks. These juicy steaks are perfect for those seeking bold, adventurous food flavors.

Servings: 4

Prepping Time: 15 minutes

Cook Time: 10 minutes

Difficulty: Easy

Ingredients:

- ✓ 4 tuna steaks
- ✓ 2 tablespoons sriracha
- ✓ 1 tablespoon soy sauce
- ✓ 1 tablespoon olive oil
- ✓ 1 tablespoon honey
- ✓ 2 cloves garlic, minced

- ✓ Salt and pepper to taste

Step-by-Step Preparation:

1. Mix Sriracha, soy sauce, olive oil, honey, garlic, salt, and pepper in a bowl.
2. Marinate the tuna steaks in the mixture for at least 10 minutes.
3. Preheat your air fryer to 400°F.
4. Cook the tuna steaks in the air fryer for 10 minutes or until the desired doneness.
5. Allow to rest for a few minutes before serving.

Nutritional Facts: (per serving)

- ❖ Calories: 250
- ❖ Protein: 35g
- ❖ Carbohydrates: 8g
- ❖ Fat: 8g
- ❖ Sodium: 600mg

This Air Fryer Spicy Sriracha Tuna Steak recipe offers a healthy yet delicious option that marries the richness of tuna with the vibrant heat of Sriracha. This tempting dish will satisfy your tastebuds, leaving you craving more. Enjoy!

Recipe 16: Healthy Fish and Chips

Kick off your healthy eating journey with this Air Fryer Healthy Fish and Chips recipe. It offers a delightful crunch to your fish and chips while cutting out the unnecessary calories of traditional deep-frying methods.

Servings: 4

Prepping Time: 15 minutes

Cook Time: 20 minutes

Difficulty: Easy

Ingredients:

- ✓ 4 white fish fillets
- ✓ 1 cup whole wheat flour
- ✓ 2 eggs, beaten
- ✓ 1 cup whole grain breadcrumbs
- ✓ 3 large potatoes, cut into chips
- ✓ 1 tbsp olive oil

- ✓ Salt and pepper to taste

Step-by-Step Preparation:

1. Preheat your air fryer to 180°C (360°F).
2. Coat the fish fillets in flour, dip them into the beaten eggs, and then into breadcrumbs.
3. Place the fish in the air fryer and cook for 10 minutes or until golden brown and crispy.
4. Toss the potato chips in olive oil, salt, and pepper.
5. Remove the fish from the air fryer, set aside, and keep warm. Put the chips in the air fryer and cook for 10 minutes until crispy.
6. Serve the fish and chips together with your favorite dipping sauce.

Nutritional Facts: (per serving)

- ❖ Calories: 350
- ❖ Protein: 30g
- ❖ Carbohydrates: 30g
- ❖ Fat: 10g
- ❖ Fiber: 4g
- ❖ Sodium: 250mg

Take delight in the unbeatable combo of this Air Fryer Healthy Fish and Chips. It's a guilt-free indulgence perfect for family dinners or casual gatherings. Enjoy this classic British dish's wonderful crunch and flavor but in a healthier, modern way!

Recipe 17: Asian-Inspired Sesame Scallops

Indulge in the flavorful blend of sesame and the sweet taste of scallops with this Air Fryer Asian-Inspired Sesame Scallops recipe. This dish is perfect for a fancy dinner at home. This dish is healthy and irresistibly delicious.

Servings: 4

Prepping Time: 15 minutes

Cook Time: 10 minutes

Difficulty: Easy

Ingredients:

- 1 lb fresh scallops
- 2 tablespoons sesame oil
- 1 tablespoon soy sauce
- 2 cloves garlic, minced
- 1 tablespoon fresh ginger, minced
- 1 tablespoon sesame seeds

- ✓ Salt and pepper to taste
- ✓ 2 green onions, chopped

Step-by-Step Preparation:

1. Pat scallops dry and season with salt and pepper.
2. Mix sesame oil, soy sauce, garlic, and ginger in a bowl.
3. Add scallops to the marinade and let it sit for 10 minutes.
4. Preheat the air fryer to 400 degrees F.
5. Place scallops in the air fryer, and cook for 10 minutes or until golden brown and firm.
6. Sprinkle with sesame seeds and chopped green onions before serving.

Nutritional Facts: (per serving)

- ❖ Calories: 172
- ❖ Fat: 9g
- ❖ Carbohydrates: 6g
- ❖ Protein: 17g
- ❖ Sodium: 820mg
- ❖ Sugar: 0g

This Air Fryer Asian-Inspired, Sesame Scallops recipe is your ticket to a savory, protein-packed meal ready in minutes. Offering a delightful blend of textures and flavors, it's a culinary experience that will transport you straight to the heart of Asia.

Recipe 18: Zesty Lemon Butter Cod

Enjoy the clean, bright flavors of this Air Fryer Zesty Lemon Butter Cod. Perfect for health-conscious eaters, this quick and straightforward meal combines the tenderness of cod with a tangy lemon butter sauce, resulting in an impressive dinner.

Servings: 4

Preparation Time: 10 minutes

Cook Time: 15 minutes

Difficulty: Easy

Ingredients:

- ✓ 4 cod fillets
- ✓ 2 tablespoons of olive oil
- ✓ 1 lemon, zested and juiced
- ✓ 2 tablespoons of butter, melted
- ✓ Salt and pepper to taste
- ✓ Chopped fresh parsley for garnish

Step-by-Step Preparation:

1. Preheat your air fryer to 400°F (200°C).
2. Pat the cod fillets dry and brush them with olive oil.
3. Season the fillets with salt, pepper, and lemon zest.
4. Place the fillets in the air fryer and cook for 10-15 minutes or until the fish flakes easily with a fork.
5. While the fish is cooking, combine the melted butter and lemon juice in a small bowl.
6. Once cooked, drizzle the fish with the lemon butter sauce and garnish with fresh parsley before serving.

Nutritional Facts: (per serving)

- ❖ Calories: 250
- ❖ Protein: 30g
- ❖ Carbs: 3g
- ❖ Fat: 12g
- ❖ Fiber: 1g
- ❖ Sugar: 1g

This Air Fryer Zesty Lemon Butter Cod is a healthy and delicious option and effortless to whip up. It's the perfect blend of tangy and savory that your taste buds will love. Once you try this recipe, your air fryer will become your go-to tool for preparing quick, flavorful meals. Enjoy!

Recipe 19: Garlic Parmesan Shrimp

Impress your dinner guests with a light and delicious appetizer that takes minimal preparation time. Air Fryer Garlic Parmesan Shrimp is a gourmet yet simple dish that blends the earthy flavor of garlic with the richness of Parmesan, leaving your palate craving more. Ideal for seafood lovers seeking healthy alternatives without sacrificing taste and texture. Let's cook up some culinary magic!

Servings: 4

Prepping Time: 10 minutes

Cook Time: 10 minutes

Difficulty: Easy

Ingredients:

- 1 pound large shrimp, peeled and deveined
- 1 tablespoon olive oil
- 4 garlic cloves, minced
- 1/2 teaspoon sea salt

- ✓ 1/4 teaspoon black pepper
- ✓ 1/4 cup grated Parmesan cheese
- ✓ 2 tablespoons chopped fresh parsley

Step-by-Step Preparation:

1. Preheat the air fryer to 400°F (200°C).
2. Combine the shrimp, olive oil, garlic, salt, and pepper in a large bowl. Toss until shrimp are well coated.
3. Place shrimp in the air fryer basket in a single layer. Cook for 5 minutes.
4. Sprinkle shrimp with Parmesan cheese and cook for 5 minutes or until golden and crispy.
5. Garnish with fresh parsley before serving.

Nutritional Facts: (per Serving)

- ❖ Calories: 205
- ❖ Fat: 7g
- ❖ Carbohydrates: 3g
- ❖ Protein: 30g

There you have it, a delectable Air Fryer Garlic Parmesan Shrimp that's both easy to make and gratifying. This dish is perfect for quick dinners, special occasions, or even as a classy appetizer. Remember, the best cooking is often the simplest. So grab your air fryer, follow this recipe, and surprise your loved ones with culinary prowess. Happy cooking!

Recipe 20: Spicy Cajun Catfish

Looking for a quick and delicious meal? Try out our Air Fryer Spicy Cajun Catfish, a dish that packs flavor and nutrition into one fantastic experience. The fusion of fresh catfish with the zest of Cajun spices brings the lively culture of Louisiana right to your plate, all without the heavy oils usually used for frying.

Servings: 4

Prepping Time: 15 minutes

Cook Time: 15 minutes

Difficulty: Easy

Ingredients:

- 4 catfish fillets
- 2 tablespoons of Cajun seasoning
- 1 teaspoon of black pepper
- 1 teaspoon of salt
- 1 tablespoon of olive oil

- ✓ 2 lemons, halved
- ✓ Fresh parsley for garnish

Step-by-Step Preparation:

1. Pat dry the catfish fillets. In a bowl, mix the Cajun seasoning, salt, and pepper.
2. Rub each fillet with the spice mix, ensuring an even coat.
3. Preheat your air fryer to 370°F (190°C).
4. Lightly brush each fillet with olive oil and place them in the air fryer.
5. Cook for 15 minutes or until the catfish is crispy and golden brown.
6. Squeeze fresh lemon juice over the cooked fillets and garnish with fresh parsley. Serve hot.

Nutritional Facts: (Per Serving)

- ❖ Calories: 220
- ❖ Total Fat: 12g
- ❖ Saturated Fat: 2.5g
- ❖ Cholesterol: 80mg
- ❖ Sodium: 640mg
- ❖ Total Carbohydrate: 1g
- ❖ Dietary Fiber: 0g
- ❖ Sugar: 0g
- ❖ Protein: 26g

Prepare to receive applause when you serve this Air Fryer Spicy Cajun Catfish. It's a simple dish that adds flavor and texture to your palate. Plus, it's a healthier alternative to traditional fried fish. Pair with a fresh salad or steamed vegetables, and you have a well-rounded meal catering to taste buds and nutritional needs. Enjoy your homemade culinary trip to Louisiana!

Chapter 3: Lean Meat and Pork

Recipe 21: Juicy Air Fryer Steak

Indulge in this mouthwatering Air Fryer Steak recipe, seasoned perfectly and cooked just right. This healthy, juicy steak is cooked to your liking in just minutes, promising a restaurant-quality meal from the comfort of your home.

Servings: 4

Prepping Time: 10 minutes

Cook Time: 15 minutes

Difficulty: Easy

Ingredients

- ✓ 4 Ribeye steaks, 1-inch thick
- ✓ 2 tablespoons of olive oil
- ✓ Salt, to taste
- ✓ Black pepper, to taste

- ✓ 2 cloves of garlic, minced
- ✓ Fresh rosemary sprigs

Step-by-Step Preparation

1. Preheat the air fryer to 400°F (200°C).
2. Pat the steaks dry with a paper towel. Rub each steak with olive oil, minced garlic, salt, and pepper on both sides.
3. Place the seasoned steaks into the air fryer basket, ensuring they aren't touching.
4. Cook the steaks for 7 minutes, then flip them over.
5. Cook for 7-8 minutes for a medium-rare finish or until the desired doneness.
6. Garnish with fresh rosemary before serving.

Nutritional Facts: (Per Serving)

- ❖ Calories: 470
- ❖ Protein: 46g
- ❖ Carbohydrates: 0g
- ❖ Fat: 30g
- ❖ Cholesterol: 120mg
- ❖ Sodium: 125mg

There you have it - a delectable, juicy Air Fryer Steak, ready in under 30 minutes. This easy yet satisfying dish is perfect for any weeknight dinner or special occasion. With a gorgeous sear and bursting with flavor, this steak will make you fall in love with air fryer cooking all over again.

Recipe 22: Herb-Crusted Pork Chops

Indulge in these Air Fryer Herb-Crusted Pork Chops, the perfect blend of savory herbs and juicy meat. Ideal for a busy weeknight dinner or casual weekend feast, these chops are a hearty meal sure to impress.

Servings: 4

Prepping Time: 15 minutes

Cook Time: 15 minutes

Difficulty: Easy

Ingredients

- ✓ 4 pork chops (bone-in)
- ✓ 1 cup bread crumbs
- ✓ 1 tablespoon chopped fresh thyme
- ✓ 1 tablespoon chopped fresh rosemary
- ✓ 1 teaspoon salt
- ✓ 1 teaspoon ground black pepper

- ✓ 2 tablespoons olive oil

Step-by-Step Preparation

1. Preheat your air fryer to 375°F (190°C).
2. Mix bread crumbs, thyme, rosemary, salt, and pepper in a bowl.
3. Brush each pork chop with olive oil, then press into the herb mixture.
4. Place the pork chops in the air fryer and cook for 15 minutes or until the internal temperature reaches 145°F (63°C).
5. Let them rest for a few minutes before serving.

Nutritional Facts: (Per Serving)

- ❖ Calories: 290
- ❖ Protein: 30g
- ❖ Carbs: 10g
- ❖ Fat: 14g

These Air Fryer Herb-Crusted Pork Chops are a delicious testament to simple, well-balanced flavors. The air fryer works wonders, delivering irresistibly crisp, golden-brown chops that are tender and juicy inside. Enjoy this gourmet experience from the comfort of your home!

Recipe 23: Healthy Air Fryer Meatloaf

Discover a healthier take on classic comfort food with our Healthy Air Fryer Meatloaf recipe. This satisfying dish brings an enticing balance of flavors and textures to your dinner table.

Servings: 4

Prepping Time: 15 minutes

Cook Time: 30 minutes

Difficulty: Easy

Ingredients:

- ✓ 1 lb lean ground turkey
- ✓ 1 small onion, finely chopped
- ✓ 2 cloves garlic, minced
- ✓ 1 carrot, grated
- ✓ 1 zucchini, grated
- ✓ 1/2 cup whole wheat breadcrumbs

- ✓ 1 egg, beaten
- ✓ 2 tablespoons ketchup
- ✓ 1 tablespoon Worcestershire sauce
- ✓ Salt and pepper to taste
- ✓ Glaze: 1/4 cup ketchup, 1 tablespoon brown sugar

Step-by-Step Preparation:

1. In a large bowl, combine turkey, onion, garlic, carrot, zucchini, breadcrumbs, egg, ketchup, Worcestershire sauce, salt, and pepper. Mix until well combined.
2. Form the mixture into a loaf that fits in your air fryer basket.
3. Cook in the air fryer at 375°F for 20 minutes.
4. Mix ketchup and brown sugar for the glaze and spread over the meatloaf.
5. Continue cooking for 10 more minutes or until the meatloaf is cooked and the glaze is caramelized.

Nutritional Facts: (per serving)

- ❖ Calories: 280
- ❖ Protein: 24g
- ❖ Carbohydrates: 20g
- ❖ Fat: 10g
- ❖ Sodium: 420mg
- ❖ Fiber: 3g

Savor this Healthy Air Fryer Meatloaf that satiates your comfort food cravings and fits into your healthy eating plan. It's a quick, easy, and delicious recipe that makes the most of your air fryer, proving that good health and good taste can go hand in hand.

Recipe 24: Rosemary-Garlic Lamb Chops

Delight your senses with this Air Fryer Rosemary-Garlic Lamb Chops recipe. It's a perfect dish for special occasions or a cozy family dinner, combining rosemary's tantalizing aroma with garlic's zesty kick to give your lamb chops a memorable flavor.

Servings: 4

Prepping Time: 15 minutes

Cook Time: 10 minutes

Difficulty: Easy

Ingredients:

- 8 lamb chops
- 3 cloves garlic, minced
- 2 tablespoons fresh rosemary, finely chopped
- 2 tablespoons olive oil
- Salt and pepper to taste

Step-by-Step Preparation:

1. Mix the minced garlic, chopped rosemary, olive oil, salt, and pepper in a bowl.
2. Marinate the lamb chops in the mixture, ensuring they're well coated. Let them sit for about 10 minutes.
3. Preheat the air fryer to 400°F (200°C).
4. Arrange the lamb chops in the air fryer and cook for 10 minutes or until desired doneness, flipping halfway through.
5. Allow the chops to rest for a few minutes before serving.

Nutritional Facts: (per serving)

- Calories: 410
- Total Fat: 25g
- Saturated Fat: 10g
- Cholesterol: 120mg
- Sodium: 100mg
- Total Carbohydrate: 1g
- Dietary Fiber: 0g
- Protein: 42g

With this Air Fryer Rosemary-Garlic Lamb Chops recipe, you're not just preparing a meal. You're creating a flavorful experience. The crisp exterior and tender inside of the lamb, combined with aromatic herbs and spices, will make your dining room feel like a high-end restaurant. So, why wait? Try it out today and surprise your family with your culinary skills!

Recipe 25: Buffalo Bison Burgers

Dive into a healthier yet delectably prosperous eating experience with our Air Fryer Buffalo Bison Burgers. Lean, protein-packed bison gets a spicy kick with buffalo sauce, offering an explosion of flavors that will leave your taste buds longing for more.

Servings: 4

Prepping Time: 15 minutes

Cook Time: 15 minutes

Difficulty: Easy

Ingredients:

- 1 lb ground bison
- 1/4 cup buffalo sauce
- Salt and pepper to taste
- 4 hamburger buns
- Lettuce, tomato, and onion for garnish
- Blue cheese or ranch dressing (optional)

Step-by-Step Preparation:

1. Preheat your air fryer to 375°F (190°C).
2. Combine the ground bison, buffalo sauce, salt, and pepper in a bowl.
3. Shape into four equal patties.
4. Place the patties in the air fryer and cook for 7 minutes.
5. Flip the burgers, then cook for another 7-8 minutes until the desired doneness.
6. Serve the bison burgers on buns with lettuce, tomato, onion, and a drizzle of blue cheese or ranch dressing.

Nutritional Facts: (per serving)

- Calories: 320
- Protein: 22g
- Fat: 18g
- Carbohydrates: 18g
- Sodium: 720mg

With this Air Fryer Buffalo Bison Burger recipe, you're creating a delicious meal and a culinary journey. Simple yet packed with flavor, these burgers offer a leaner alternative to traditional beef without compromising taste. They're quick, easy, and sure to be a hit at your next barbecue or family dinner!

Recipe 26: Asian Glazed Pork Tenderloin

Delve into the succulent and aromatic flavors of Air Fryer Asian Glazed Pork Tenderloin, a delightful dish that will make your dinner special. Juicy pork tenderloin glazed with a tangy, sweet Asian sauce, then air-fried to perfection—a gastronomic adventure that's both satisfying and nutritious.

Servings: 4

Prepping Time: 15 minutes

Cook Time: 25 minutes

Difficulty: Medium

Ingredients:

- ✓ 1 lb pork tenderloin
- ✓ 2 cloves garlic, minced
- ✓ 2 tablespoons soy sauce
- ✓ 2 tablespoons honey
- ✓ 1 tablespoon sesame oil
- ✓ 1 tablespoon grated fresh ginger

- ✓ 1 teaspoon chili flakes (optional)
- ✓ Salt and pepper to taste
- ✓ Green onions and sesame seeds for garnish

Step-by-Step Preparation:

1. Mix minced garlic, soy sauce, honey, sesame oil, ginger, chili flakes, salt, and pepper to glaze in a bowl.
2. Marinate the pork tenderloin in the glaze for at least 30 minutes or overnight.
3. Preheat the air fryer to 375°F.
4. Cook the pork tenderloin in the air fryer for 25 minutes or until the internal temperature reaches 145°F.
5. Let it rest for a few minutes before slicing. Drizzle with leftover glaze, garnish with green onions and sesame seeds.

Nutritional Facts: (per serving)

- ❖ Calories: 275
- ❖ Fat: 11g
- ❖ Carbohydrates: 12g
- ❖ Protein: 32g
- ❖ Fiber: 2g
- ❖ Sugar: 8g
- ❖ Cholesterol: 90mg
- ❖ Sodium: 750mg

Our Air Fryer Asian Glazed Pork Tenderloin is a feast of flavors in a dish, bringing restaurant-quality dining to your table. It's easy, healthy, and perfect for a weeknight dinner or a special occasion. Try it today and add an exciting new recipe to your culinary repertoire.

Recipe 27: BBQ Pulled Pork

Experience the delight of a homemade BBQ pulled pork meal with the help of your Air Fryer. This recipe combines savory, smoky, and tender pulled pork, a sure-fire hit for any BBQ lover.

Servings: 6

Prepping Time: 15 minutes

Cook Time: 4 hours

Difficulty: Intermediate

Ingredients:

- ✓ 2 lbs pork shoulder
- ✓ 1 cup BBQ sauce
- ✓ 1/2 cup brown sugar
- ✓ 1/4 cup apple cider vinegar
- ✓ 1 tablespoon smoked paprika
- ✓ 1 tablespoon garlic powder

- ✓ Salt and pepper to taste

Step-by-Step Preparation:

1. Mix brown sugar, smoked paprika, garlic powder, salt, and pepper in a bowl.
2. Rub this mixture all over the pork shoulder.
3. Place the pork in the Air Fryer and cook at 180°F for 4 hours.
4. Once done, let it rest for 10 minutes.
5. Shred the pork using two forks, then mix in BBQ sauce and apple cider vinegar.
6. Return the mixture to the Air Fryer and cook for another 5 minutes at 350°F.

Nutritional Facts: (Per Serving)

- ❖ Calories: 380
- ❖ Protein: 35g
- ❖ Carbs: 18g
- ❖ Fat: 18g
- ❖ Fiber: 1g
- ❖ Sugar: 15g

There you have it. Your mouthwatering Air Fryer BBQ Pulled Pork. This recipe's flavors are deeply satisfying and incredibly comforting. It's perfect for a weekend BBQ party or a simple family dinner. Enjoy!

Recipe 28: Air Fried Veal Scallopini

This tantalizing Air Fried Veal Scallopini recipe is a delicious blend of traditional Italian cuisine with a modern, healthy twist. Light yet fulfilling, the air fryer ensures tender veal while minimizing oil usage.

Servings: 4

Prepping Time: 15 minutes

Cook Time: 15 minutes

Difficulty: Moderate

Ingredients

- ✓ 4 veal cutlets (around 1 pound)
- ✓ 1/2 cup flour
- ✓ 2 eggs, beaten
- ✓ 1 cup panko breadcrumbs
- ✓ Salt and pepper to taste
- ✓ 1 lemon, sliced for garnish

- ✓ Fresh parsley, chopped for garnish

Step-by-Step Preparation

1. Preheat your air fryer to 400°F.
2. Season the veal cutlets with salt and pepper.
3. Dredge each cutlet in flour, dip in the beaten eggs, and coat in breadcrumbs.
4. Place the cutlets in the air fryer and cook for 7-8 minutes until golden and crispy on each side.
5. Let it rest for a few minutes before serving. Garnish with lemon slices and fresh parsley.

Nutritional Facts: (Per Serving)

- ❖ Calories: 300 kcal
- ❖ Protein: 32 g
- ❖ Fat: 8 g
- ❖ Carbohydrates: 22 g
- ❖ Fiber: 1 g
- ❖ Sugar: 1 g

This Air Fried Veal Scallopini delivers an unforgettable dining experience, marrying the classic flavors of Italy with the benefits of air frying. Perfect for a family dinner or special occasion, this dish proves that delicious doesn't have to mean complicated or unhealthy. Enjoy this elegant meal tonight!

Recipe 29: Spicy Italian Sausage Links

Experience an explosion of flavor with Air Fryer Spicy Italian Sausage Links. These juicy, well-seasoned links deliver just the right spice, making them the perfect addition to any meal or as a tasty appetizer.

Servings: 4

Prepping Time: 10 minutes

Cook Time: 15 minutes

Difficulty: Easy

Ingredients:

- ✓ 4 Spicy Italian sausage links
- ✓ 2 tbsp olive oil
- ✓ 1 tbsp Italian seasoning
- ✓ 1 tsp garlic powder
- ✓ 1 tsp onion powder
- ✓ 1 tsp paprika

- ✓ Salt and pepper to taste

Step-by-Step Preparation:

1. Preheat the air fryer to 380°F for about 5 minutes.
2. Rub the sausages with olive oil while preheating and combine Italian seasoning, garlic powder, onion powder, paprika, salt, and pepper.
3. Arrange the sausages in the air fryer basket, ensuring they don't touch.
4. Air fry for 15 minutes, flipping halfway through.
5. Allow to rest for 2-3 minutes before serving.

Nutritional Facts: (Per serving)

- ❖ Calories: 310
- ❖ Total Fat: 23g
- ❖ Saturated Fat: 8g
- ❖ Cholesterol: 60mg
- ❖ Sodium: 790mg
- ❖ Total Carbohydrates: 3g
- ❖ Dietary Fiber: 1g
- ❖ Sugars: 1g
- ❖ Protein: 22g

There you have it, Air Fryer Spicy Italian Sausage Links that will satisfy your cravings. They are easy to prepare, rich in flavors, and wonderfully juicy. Pair them with your favorite side dish, or enjoy them as is for a delicious, protein-packed meal.

Recipe 30: Healthy Turkey Bacon

Tantalize your taste buds with this healthier version of classic bacon. Made in an air fryer, this Turkey Bacon offers all the crispiness and flavor you love while cutting down on fats and sodium. It's a delightful and guilt-free addition to any meal.

Servings: 4

Prepping Time: 5 minutes

Cook Time: 10 minutes

Difficulty: Easy

Ingredients:

- ✓ 8 slices of Turkey Bacon

Step-by-Step Preparation:

1. Preheat your air fryer to 400°F (200°C).
2. Arrange the turkey bacon slices in the air fryer basket, ensuring they don't overlap.

3. Cook for 10 minutes or until the bacon reaches your desired crispiness.
4. Carefully remove the turkey bacon from the air fryer, allowing them to cool slightly before serving.

Nutritional Facts: (Per serving)

- Calories: 60
- Fat: 3g
- Saturated Fat: 1g
- Cholesterol: 30mg
- Sodium: 180mg
- Carbohydrates: 0g
- Fiber: 0g
- Sugar: 0g
- Protein: 8g

This air fryer turkey bacon is a simple and healthier alternative to traditional bacon, perfect for breakfast, lunch, or a savory snack. Ready in minutes, it's a must-try for everyone looking to add a bit of crunch to their diet without the extra guilt. Enjoy the sizzle and taste of bacon, made light and easy.

Chapter 4: Plant-based Protein Dishes

Recipe 31: Crispy Tofu Nuggets

Looking for a healthier twist on traditional nuggets? Try these delicious Air Fryer Crispy Tofu Nuggets. They're perfect for those following a plant-based diet and appealing to kids and adults alike. Enjoy them as an appetizer or a protein-packed snack.

Servings: 4

Prepping Time: 15 minutes

Cook Time: 15 minutes

Difficulty: Easy

Ingredients:

- ✓ 14 oz of firm tofu
- ✓ 1/2 cup of panko breadcrumbs
- ✓ 1/4 cup of cornstarch
- ✓ 1/2 teaspoon of garlic powder

- ✓ 1/2 teaspoon of onion powder
- ✓ 1/2 teaspoon of paprika
- ✓ Salt and pepper to taste
- ✓ Olive oil spray

Step-by-Step Preparation:

1. Press the tofu for 15 minutes to remove excess water. Cut into nugget-sized pieces.
2. Mix panko breadcrumbs, cornstarch, garlic powder, onion powder, paprika, salt, and pepper in a bowl.
3. Coat each tofu nugget thoroughly with the breadcrumb mixture.
4. Arrange the nuggets in the air fryer basket in a single layer. Spray lightly with olive oil.
5. Air fry at 400°F for 15 minutes, flipping halfway through, until golden and crispy.

Nutritional Facts: (Per serving)

- ❖ Calories: 140
- ❖ Protein: 9g
- ❖ Carbs: 15g
- ❖ Fiber: 1g
- ❖ Fat: 5g

There you have it, guilt-free Air Fryer Crispy Tofu Nuggets. With the right balance of crispiness and flavorful seasoning, they're guaranteed to be a hit at your next gathering or family dinner. Enjoy this healthier alternative to classic nuggets with your favorite dip or as a main course addition.

Recipe 32: Spicy Chickpea Patties

Get ready to enjoy Air Fryer Spicy Chickpea Patties - a delightful blend of health and taste. These protein-packed patties are bursting with savory spices, offering a simple yet satisfying meatless meal that is sure to impress.

Servings: 4

Prepping Time: 15 minutes

Cook Time: 20 minutes

Difficulty: Easy

Ingredients:

- ✓ 2 cups cooked chickpeas
- ✓ 1 red onion, finely chopped
- ✓ 2 cloves of garlic, minced
- ✓ 2 tablespoons olive oil
- ✓ 1 teaspoon cumin
- ✓ 1 teaspoon coriander

- ✓ 1/2 teaspoon cayenne pepper
- ✓ Salt to taste
- ✓ 2 tablespoons parsley, finely chopped
- ✓ 1 cup breadcrumbs

Step-by-Step Preparation:

1. Combine chickpeas, onion, garlic, spices, and parsley until smooth in a food processor.
2. Form the mixture into patties and coat each with breadcrumbs.
3. Preheat the air fryer to 375°F.
4. Brush each patty with olive oil, then place in the air fryer.
5. Cook for 10 minutes, flip, then cook for 10 minutes until golden brown.

Nutritional Facts: (Per serving)

- ❖ Calories: 298
- ❖ Protein: 9g
- ❖ Fat: 8g
- ❖ Carbs: 49g
- ❖ Fiber: 9g
- ❖ Sugar: 6g

These Air Fryer Spicy Chickpea Patties are an excellent addition to your weekly meal plan. They're great on buns with your favorite toppings or served with a side salad for a lighter meal. Quick, tasty, and nutritionally balanced – a perfect meat-free choice for any day.

Recipe 33: Air Fryer Falafel

Prepare to savor a classic Middle Eastern delight, the Air Fryer Falafel. This delicious and healthy plant-based recipe gives you perfectly crispy falafel with less oil, maintaining all the rich, herby flavors you love and a crunchy exterior with a soft, flavorful center.

Servings: 4

Prepping Time: 15 minutes

Cook Time: 15 minutes

Difficulty: Easy

Ingredients:

- ✓ 2 cups canned chickpeas, drained
- ✓ 1 large onion, chopped
- ✓ 2 cloves of garlic, minced
- ✓ 1 cup fresh parsley
- ✓ 1 cup fresh cilantro
- ✓ 1 teaspoon salt

- ✓ 1/2 teaspoon pepper
- ✓ 2 teaspoons cumin
- ✓ 1 teaspoon coriander
- ✓ 1 teaspoon baking powder
- ✓ 1/2 cup all-purpose flour
- ✓ Cooking spray

Step-by-Step Preparation:

1. Combine chickpeas, onion, garlic, parsley, cilantro, salt, pepper, cumin, and coriander in a food processor. Process until blended but not pureed.
2. Sprinkle in the baking powder and half of the flour, and pulse. Add more flour until the mixture forms a small ball.
3. Shape the mixture into small patties using your hands.
4. Preheat the air fryer to 375°F. Prepare the falafel with cooking spray in the air fryer basket.
5. Cook for 15 minutes, flipping halfway, until golden brown and crispy.

Nutritional Facts: (Per serving)

- ❖ Calories: 256
- ❖ Protein: 12g
- ❖ Carbohydrates: 44g
- ❖ Fat: 4g
- ❖ Sodium: 701mg
- ❖ Fiber: 9g

These Air Fryer falafels will transport you straight to the bustling streets of the Middle East. Crispy, hearty, and brimming with flavors, they are a guilt-free treat that pairs perfectly with a tangy tahini sauce or nestled in a warm pita. Enjoy this healthy, vegetarian-friendly feast from your very own kitchen.

Recipe 34: Tempeh Bacon Bits

Savor the delightful crunch and smoky flavor of Air Fryer Tempeh Bacon Bits. This vegetarian treat perfectly mimics the crispiness of real bacon bits but with less fat and more protein. Ideal for salad toppings, garnishing, or a protein-packed snack, these tiny flavorful nuggets are easy to prepare and surprisingly satisfying.

Servings: 4

Prepping Time: 10 minutes

Cook Time: 15 minutes

Difficulty: Easy

Ingredients:

- 8 oz tempeh
- 2 tbsp soy sauce
- 1 tbsp maple syrup
- 1 tsp liquid smoke
- 1/2 tsp garlic powder

- ✓ 1/2 tsp smoked paprika
- ✓ 1 tbsp olive oil

Step-by-Step Preparation:

1. Cut tempeh into small cubes.
2. Mix a bowl of soy sauce, maple syrup, liquid smoke, garlic powder, and smoked paprika.
3. Add tempeh cubes and toss to coat. Let it marinate for 10 minutes.
4. Preheat your air fryer to 370°F (188°C).
5. Drizzle olive oil over marinated tempeh and toss to coat evenly.
6. Air fry for 15 minutes, shaking occasionally for even cooking.

Nutritional Facts: (Per serving)

- ❖ Calories: 180
- ❖ Protein: 12g
- ❖ Fat: 10g
- ❖ Carbohydrates: 13g
- ❖ Fiber: 1g
- ❖ Sugar: 4g

Air Fryer Tempeh Bacon Bits make a versatile and nutritious meal addition. They offer a unique twist to traditional bacon, reducing fats while keeping the desirable crunch and flavor intact. From salads to sandwiches and baked potatoes, these delicious bites satisfy your craving for that meaty savor without straying from a healthy, plant-based diet.

Recipe 35: Edamame and Quinoa Burgers

Savor the nutritious goodness of plant-based Air Fryer Edamame and Quinoa Burgers. Easy to make, they're a delightful mix of protein-rich quinoa and edamame, brimming with flavors from herbs and spices, and have an irresistible crunchy exterior.

Servings: 4

Prepping Time: 20 minutes

Cook Time: 20 minutes

Difficulty: Easy

Ingredients

- ✓ 1 cup cooked quinoa
- ✓ 2 cups shelled edamame
- ✓ 1 small onion, finely diced
- ✓ 2 garlic cloves, minced
- ✓ 1/2 cup breadcrumbs
- ✓ 1 egg (or flax egg for the vegan option)

- ✓ Salt and pepper to taste
- ✓ Olive oil for brushing
- ✓ 4 burger buns
- ✓ Your favorite burger toppings

Step-by-Step Preparation

1. In a food processor, pulse edamame until roughly chopped.
2. Add the cooked quinoa, onion, garlic, breadcrumbs, egg, salt, and pepper. Process until well combined.
3. Shape the mixture into 4 patties.
4. Preheat the air fryer to 375°F.
5. Brush each patty with olive oil and air fry for 10 minutes.
6. Serve on burger buns with your favorite toppings.

Nutritional Facts: (Per serving)

- ❖ Calories: 325
- ❖ Protein: 15g
- ❖ Carbs: 45g
- ❖ Fat: 9g
- ❖ Fiber: 10g

Whether you're a vegetarian, a health enthusiast, or simply a lover of tasty food, these Air Fryer Edamame and Quinoa Burgers are an absolute must-try. Ready in under an hour, they make a wholesome meal that satiates the palate while offering nourishing benefits.

Recipe 36: Crispy Seitan 'Chicken' Tenders

Unleash the power of your air fryer to make these mouthwatering Crispy Seitan 'Chicken' Tenders. A perfect vegan alternative to traditional chicken tenders that packs an incredible punch of taste and crunch!

Servings: 4

Prepping Time: 30 minutes

Cook Time: 15 minutes

Difficulty: Medium

Ingredients:

- ✓ 1 pound of seitan, cut into strips
- ✓ 1 cup of almond milk
- ✓ 1 cup of all-purpose flour
- ✓ 1 cup of panko breadcrumbs
- ✓ 1 tablespoon of smoked paprika
- ✓ Salt and pepper to taste

- ✓ Cooking spray

Step-by-Step Preparation:

1. Dip seitan strips in almond milk, then coat with flour.
2. Combine panko breadcrumbs with smoked paprika, salt, and pepper.
3. Roll seitan strips in the breadcrumb mixture.
4. Spray the air fryer basket with cooking spray, then arrange seitan strips, ensuring they don't overlap.
5. Cook at 400°F for 15 minutes or until golden and crispy, turning halfway through.

Nutritional Facts: (Per serving)

- ❖ Calories: 260
- ❖ Total Fat: 3g
- ❖ Saturated Fat: 0g
- ❖ Trans Fat: 0g
- ❖ Cholesterol: 0mg
- ❖ Sodium: 450mg
- ❖ Total Carbohydrate: 30g
- ❖ Dietary Fiber: 4g
- ❖ Total Sugars: 1g
- ❖ Protein: 30g

These Air Fryer Crispy Seitan 'Chicken' Tenders are a culinary delight that even meat-eaters will love. Crispy on the outside, tender on the inside, and utterly delicious make for a fantastic appetizer or main dish for any occasion. Vegan cooking has never been more tempting!

Recipe 37: Sweet and Spicy Tofu Stir Fry

Revamp your vegan dining experience with this delectable Air Fryer Sweet and Spicy Tofu Stir Fry. Crispy tofu tossed in a succulent sauce infused with a perfect balance of sweet and spicy flavors - this is a treat that will tantalize your tastebuds!

Servings: 4

Prepping Time: 15 minutes

Cook Time: 20 minutes

Difficulty: Easy

Ingredients

- ✓ 400g Extra firm tofu
- ✓ 1 cup Mixed bell peppers
- ✓ 1 Onion, chopped
- ✓ 2 cloves Garlic, minced
- ✓ 2 tbsp Soy sauce
- ✓ 1 tbsp Sriracha

- ✓ 2 tbsp Honey
- ✓ 1 tbsp Cornstarch
- ✓ 1/2 cup Water
- ✓ 2 tbsp Vegetable oil
- ✓ Salt and pepper to taste

Step-by-Step Preparation

1. Press tofu to remove excess water and cut it into cubes.
2. Air fry the tofu cubes at 375F for 15 minutes or until crispy.
3. While tofu is frying, sauté onion, bell peppers, and Garlic in oil.
4. Mix soy sauce, sriracha, honey, cornstarch, and water to create the sauce.
5. Add the air-fried tofu to the sautéed veggies, pour the sauce, and toss until well coated.
6. Cook for a further 5 minutes until the sauce thickens. Season with salt and pepper.

Nutritional Facts: (Per serving)

- ❖ Calories: 210
- ❖ Fat: 10g
- ❖ Protein: 14g
- ❖ Carbohydrates: 20g
- ❖ Sugar: 8g
- ❖ Fiber: 2g
- ❖ Sodium: 430mg

With the Air Fryer Sweet and Spicy Tofu Stir Fry, you've just discovered a guilt-free delight that is not only packed with plant-based protein but is also explosively flavorful. It's ideal for a quick weeknight dinner, impressing your guests, or when you need spicy-sweet comfort food.

Recipe 38: Crunchy Lentil Fritters

Indulge in the crunchy delight of Air Fryer Lentil Fritters, a healthy snack perfect for any occasion. These cakes are packed with protein, incredibly tasty, and effortlessly made in your air fryer.

Servings: 4

Prepping Time: 15 minutes

Cook Time: 20 minutes

Difficulty: Easy

Ingredients:

- 1 cup lentils (soaked overnight)
- 1 onion (finely chopped)
- 2 green chilies (finely chopped)
- 2 tablespoons fresh coriander (finely chopped)
- 1 teaspoon cumin seeds
- Salt to taste

- ✓ 1/4 teaspoon turmeric powder
- ✓ 2 teaspoons vegetable oil for brushing

Step-by-Step Preparation:

1. Drain lentils and grind them in a food processor until they form a coarse paste.
2. Combine the lentil paste, onion, chilies, coriander, cumin seeds, salt, and turmeric in a mixing bowl.
3. Preheat your air fryer to 180°C (350°F).
4. Shape the lentil mixture into small flat fritters and lightly brush each with oil.
5. Place the fritters in the air fryer basket, leaving some space between them.
6. Cook for 10 minutes, then flip and cook for another 10 minutes or until they turn golden brown.

Nutritional Facts: (Per serving)

- ❖ Calories: 200
- ❖ Protein: 13g
- ❖ Carbs: 32g
- ❖ Fat: 3g
- ❖ Fiber: 10g
- ❖ Sodium: 240mg

Enjoy these delicious, crunchy lentil cakes straight out of the air fryer. They're bursting with flavors and a guilt-free, high-protein choice for health-conscious snackers. Serve hot with a spicy dip or chutney, and relish this delectable delight.

Recipe 39: Air Fried Black Bean Taquitos

Dive into the delicious world of Mexican cuisine with these homemade Air Fried Black Bean Taquitos. These are light, crispy, and packed with flavors, perfect for a quick lunch or a crowd-pleasing appetizer for your next gathering.

Servings: 4

Prepping Time: 15 minutes

Cook Time: 10 minutes

Difficulty: Easy

Ingredients:

- ✓ 2 cups of canned black beans, drained and rinsed
- ✓ 1 cup of shredded cheese (Cheddar/Mexican blend)
- ✓ 1/2 cup of red onion, chopped
- ✓ 1/2 cup of corn kernels, canned/drained or fresh
- ✓ 1 tsp of ground cumin
- ✓ 1/2 tsp of chili powder

- ✓ Salt and pepper to taste
- ✓ 8 small flour tortillas
- ✓ Cooking spray

Step-by-Step Preparation:

1. Combine black beans, cheese, onion, corn, cumin, chili powder, salt, and pepper in a large bowl.
2. Lay out the tortillas and divide the mixture evenly among them.
3. Roll each tortilla tightly, and secure it with a toothpick if necessary.
4. Preheat the air fryer to 400°F (200°C).
5. Spray the taquitos lightly with cooking spray and place them in the air fryer.
6. Cook for 10 minutes until golden and crispy, turning halfway through.
7. Allow them to cool slightly before serving with your favorite dip.

Nutritional Facts: (Per serving)

- ❖ Calories: 365
- ❖ Total Fat: 11g
- ❖ Saturated Fat: 5g
- ❖ Cholesterol: 30mg
- ❖ Sodium: 650mg
- ❖ Total Carbohydrate: 50g
- ❖ Dietary Fiber: 7g
- ❖ Total Sugars: 3g
- ❖ Protein: 17g

These Air Fried Black Bean Taquitos will surely be a hit, providing a satisfying crunch with every bite. They are straightforward to make, packed with nutritious ingredients, and lower in fat than traditional deep-fried versions. Enjoy this guilt-free delight at your next family dinner or party!

Recipe 40: BBQ Jackfruit Pulled Pork

Satisfy your plant-based craving with this delightful Air Fryer BBQ Jackfruit 'Pulled Pork.' This dish offers a meat-free, satisfying twist that is perfect for vegans and meat lovers alike.

Servings: 4

Prepping Time: 10 minutes

Cook Time: 20 minutes

Difficulty: Easy

Ingredients

- ✓ 2 cans (20 oz each) of young green jackfruit in water
- ✓ 1 tablespoon olive oil
- ✓ 1 small onion, chopped
- ✓ 2 cloves garlic, minced
- ✓ 1 cup barbecue sauce
- ✓ Salt and pepper to taste

Step-by-Step Preparation

1. Drain and rinse the jackfruit, pat it dry, and shred it into thin strands.
2. Set your air fryer to preheat at 350°F.
3. Mix the shredded jackfruit, chopped onion, minced garlic, and barbecue sauce in a bowl.
4. Transfer the mixture to the air fryer and cook for 20 minutes, shaking halfway through.
5. Season with salt and pepper and serve with your favorite side dish.

Nutritional Facts: (Per serving)

- Calories: 215
- Protein: 2.6g
- Fat: 3.8g
- Carbohydrates: 45g
- Fiber: 5g
- Sodium: 465mg

Next time you yearn for some BBQ, this Air Fryer BBQ Jackfruit 'Pulled Pork' is the way to go. Not only is it packed with flavor, but it also provides a healthier alternative to traditional BBQ pulled pork. Perfect for your next cookout or family dinner, it's a versatile dish that everyone will enjoy.

Chapter 5: Protein-Packed Eggs & Dairy

Recipe 41: Air Fryer Omelette Cups

Start your day with this simple and nutritious Air Fryer Omelette Cups recipe. These cups are a fun, personalized breakfast option that will impress your family and friends, and the best part is that they are super easy to make in your air fryer.

Servings: 6

Prepping Time: 10 minutes

Cook Time: 15 minutes

Difficulty: Easy

Ingredients:

- 6 eggs
- 1/4 cup milk
- Salt and pepper to taste
- 1/2 cup shredded cheddar cheese

- ✓ 1/4 cup diced bell peppers
- ✓ 1/4 cup diced onions
- ✓ 1/4 cup diced ham

Step-by-Step Preparation:

1. Whisk together eggs, milk, salt, and pepper in a bowl.
2. Grease a 6-cup muffin tin and divide the diced vegetables and ham evenly among the cups.
3. Pour the egg mixture into each cup, filling them 3/4 of the way.
4. Sprinkle shredded cheese on top.
5. Place the muffin tin in the air fryer basket. Cook at 350°F for 15 minutes or until eggs are set.
6. Let cool for a few minutes before removing from the tin.

Nutritional Facts: (Per serving)

- ❖ Calories: 140
- ❖ Protein: 11g
- ❖ Carbohydrates: 3g
- ❖ Fat: 9g
- ❖ Cholesterol: 190mg
- ❖ Sodium: 300mg

Air Fryer Omelette Cups are a great way to start your day. They are nutritious and tasty and can be made ahead of time for those busy mornings. Mix up the ingredients to create your personalized cup every time. This versatile recipe is an excellent addition to your breakfast repertoire.

Recipe 42: Mozzarella Sticks

Introduce your tastebuds to the classic delight of mozzarella sticks without any guilt. With the help of an air fryer, you can achieve crispy, melty cheese sticks that are perfect for a snack or appetizer.

Servings: 4

Prepping Time: 10 minutes

Cook Time: 10 minutes

Difficulty: Easy

Ingredients:

- 12 mozzarella string cheese sticks
- 1 cup flour
- 2 eggs, beaten
- 2 cups Italian breadcrumbs
- Nonstick cooking spray

Step-by-Step Preparation:

1. Freeze mozzarella sticks for at least 2 hours.
2. Preheat your air fryer to 370°F (190°C).
3. Dredge each stick in flour, egg, and breadcrumbs. Repeat the egg and breadcrumbs steps for a thick coating.
4. Place the coated sticks in a single layer in the air fryer, and spray lightly with nonstick cooking spray.
5. Cook for 5 minutes, flip, then cook for another 5 minutes or until golden brown. Serve hot with marinara sauce.

Nutritional Facts: (Per serving)

- Calories: 200
- Fat: 12g
- Carbs: 13g
- Protein: 10g

Enjoy the mouthwatering combination of crunchy and creamy that only homemade mozzarella sticks can offer. These treats will leave everyone at your table reaching for more, making them the perfect addition to any party or a cozy movie night at home.

Recipe 43: Quiche Lorraine Bites

Indulge in the timeless charm of French cuisine with our mini Quiche Lorraine Bites. These delicious morsels cooked in an air fryer offer a healthy, low-fuss brunch option that's big on flavor and elegance.

- **Servings:** 24 bites
- **Prepping Time:** 20 minutes
- **Cook Time:** 15 minutes
- **Difficulty:** Medium

Ingredients:

- ✓ 1 roll of refrigerated pie crust
- ✓ 6 large eggs
- ✓ 1 cup heavy cream
- ✓ 1 cup grated Gruyere cheese
- ✓ 1/2 cup chopped cooked bacon
- ✓ Salt and pepper to taste

Step-by-Step Preparation:

1. Roll out the pie crust and cut out 24 circles. Press each into the cups of a mini muffin pan.
2. Mix eggs, cream, cheese, bacon, salt, and pepper in a bowl.
3. Spoon the mixture into the crust-lined cups.
4. Cook in the air fryer at 350°F for 15 minutes or until the quiches are set and lightly browned.
5. Allow to cool slightly before serving.

Nutritional Facts: (Per bite)

- Calories: 95
- Carbs: 6g
- Protein: 3g
- Fat: 7g
- Fiber: 0g
- Sodium: 120mg

These bite-sized Quiche Lorraine offer a delightful spin on the classic recipe. Air-fried to perfection, they present a delicious and innovative way to entertain at brunch or to enjoy as a savory snack. Bon appétit!

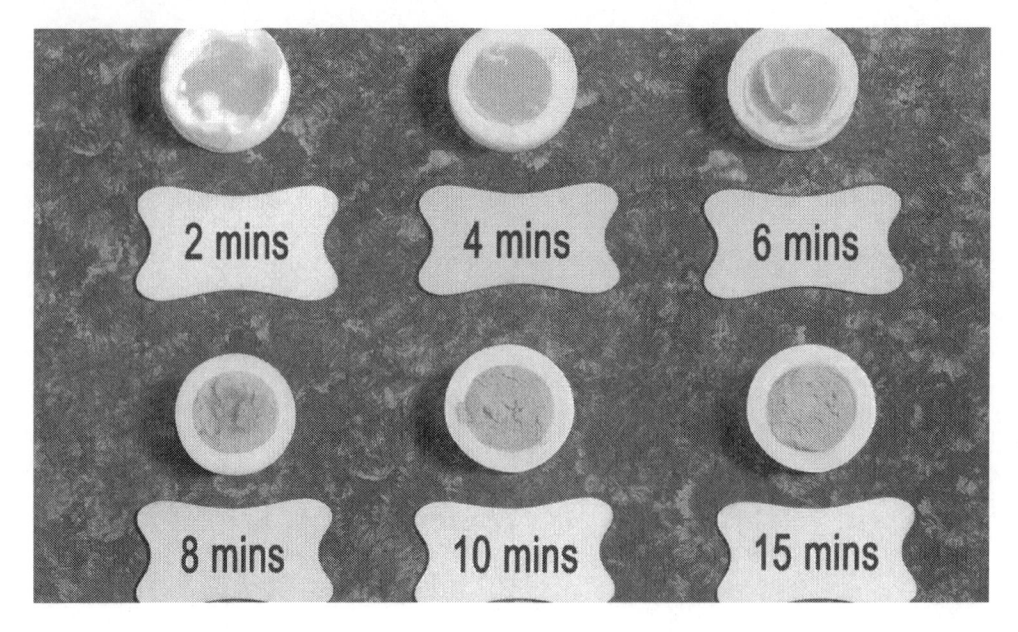

Recipe 44: Parmesan Crusted Hard-Boiled Eggs

Savor a twist on classic deviled eggs with Air Fryer Parmesan Crusted Hard-Boiled Eggs. Infusing an aromatic blend of spices and a golden Parmesan crust, this dish is perfect for entertaining guests or adding a delicious snack.

Servings: 6

Prepping Time: 10 minutes

Cook Time: 15 minutes

Difficulty: Easy

Ingredients:

- ✓ 6 hard-boiled eggs
- ✓ ½ cup Parmesan cheese, grated
- ✓ 1 cup Panko breadcrumbs
- ✓ ½ tsp garlic powder
- ✓ ½ tsp paprika

- ✓ 2 beaten eggs
- ✓ Salt and pepper to taste

Step-by-Step Preparation:

1. Preheat your air fryer to 375°F.
2. Peel the hard-boiled eggs and set aside.
3. Combine Parmesan cheese, breadcrumbs, garlic powder, paprika, salt, and pepper in a bowl.
4. Dip each hard-boiled egg into the beaten eggs, then roll in the breadcrumb mixture.
5. Place the crusted eggs in the air fryer basket and cook for 15 minutes, until golden brown.
6. Let them cool before serving.

Nutritional Facts: (Per serving)

- ❖ Calories: 215
- ❖ Fat: 12g
- ❖ Carbohydrates: 14g
- ❖ Protein: 12g
- ❖ Fiber: 1g
- ❖ Sugar: 2g
- ❖ Sodium: 425mg

These Air Fryer Parmesan Crusted Hard-Boiled Eggs are an irresistible blend of flavor, texture, and nutrition. Their simplicity and speed of preparation make them perfect for parties, picnics, or just a healthy snack on the go. Enjoy them today and taste the difference.

Recipe 45: Air Fryer Frittata with Spinach and Feta

Start your day with a nutritious Air Fryer Frittata with Spinach and Feta. It's a great way to incorporate veggies into your breakfast, and it's so flavorful you won't believe it's low-carb!

Servings: 4

Prepping Time: 10 minutes

Cook Time: 15 minutes

Difficulty: Easy

Ingredients:

- 6 large eggs
- 1/2 cup spinach, chopped
- 1/4 cup feta cheese, crumbled
- 1/4 cup milk
- 1 small onion, diced

- ✓ 1/2 teaspoon salt
- ✓ 1/4 teaspoon pepper

Step-by-Step Preparation:

1. In a bowl, beat the eggs, milk, salt, and pepper until well combined.
2. Stir in the spinach, feta cheese, and diced onion.
3. Pour the mixture into a greased air fryer-safe pan.
4. Cook in the air fryer at 350°F for 15 minutes or until the frittata is set and golden brown.
5. Let it cool for a few minutes before slicing and serving.

Nutritional Facts per Serving:

- ❖ Calories: 140
- ❖ Carbs: 2g
- ❖ Protein: 10g
- ❖ Fat: 10g
- ❖ Sodium: 340mg
- ❖ Fiber: 1g

Enjoy this delicious and nutritious Air Fryer Frittata with Spinach and Feta, a perfect option for a high-protein, low-carb diet. Quick and easy to prepare, it's ideal for busy weekday breakfasts or laid-back weekend brunches. Give it a try and taste the goodness!

Recipe 46: Greek Yogurt Marinated Chicken

Introduce the irresistible flavor of Greece to your kitchen with this Air Fryer Greek Yogurt Marinated Chicken recipe. Experience the Mediterranean's aromatic herbs and creamy yogurt in a delightfully easy yet satisfying meal that will impress you.

Servings: 4

Prepping Time: 15 minutes plus marinating time (minimum 2 hours)

Cook Time: 25 minutes

Difficulty: Easy

Ingredients:

- ✓ 4 chicken breasts
- ✓ 1 cup Greek yogurt
- ✓ 2 cloves garlic, minced
- ✓ 1 tbsp olive oil
- ✓ 1 lemon, zest, and juice
- ✓ 2 tsp dried oregano

- ✓ 1/2 tsp salt
- ✓ 1/4 tsp black pepper

Step-by-Step Preparation:

1. Combine Greek yogurt, minced garlic, olive oil, lemon zest, juice, dried oregano, salt, and pepper in a bowl.
2. Add the chicken breasts to the bowl and coat them evenly with the marinade. Cover and refrigerate for at least 2 hours.
3. Preheat your air fryer to 375°F (190°C).
4. Place the marinated chicken breasts in the air fryer. Cook for 25 minutes or until the chicken is golden brown.

Nutritional Facts: (Per serving)

- ❖ Calories: 250
- ❖ Protein: 36g
- ❖ Carbs: 4g
- ❖ Fat: 10g

This Air Fryer Greek Yogurt Marinated Chicken recipe brings a dash of Greek sunshine into your home, ensuring a wholesome and flavorful meal. Whether for a weeknight dinner or a casual gathering, this dish promises to deliver a savory experience that makes healthy eating a joy.

Recipe 47: Eggplant Parmesan Stacks

Enjoy a healthy take on Italian cuisine with Air Fryer Eggplant Parmesan Stacks. This recipe offers a mouthwatering fusion of crunchy eggplant slices and rich, gooey cheese, achieved without excess oil.

Servings: 4

Prepping Time: 20 minutes

Cook Time: 15 minutes

Difficulty: Easy

Ingredients:

- ✓ 1 large eggplant
- ✓ 2 eggs
- ✓ 1 cup breadcrumbs
- ✓ 1/2 cup Parmesan cheese, grated
- ✓ 1 cup mozzarella cheese, shredded
- ✓ 2 cups marinara sauce

- ✓ Salt and pepper to taste
- ✓ Fresh basil leaves for garnish

Step-by-Step Preparation:

1. Slice the eggplant into half-inch thick rounds. Sprinkle with salt and let sit for 10 minutes.
2. Rinse eggplant slices and pat dry. Dip each slice into beaten eggs, then coat with breadcrumbs and Parmesan.
3. Place the coated eggplant slices in the air fryer and cook at 375°F for 10 minutes.
4. Layer each eggplant slice with marinara sauce and mozzarella, then cook for another 5 minutes or until the cheese is melted and bubbly.
5. Garnish with fresh basil leaves and serve hot.

Nutritional Facts: (Per serving)

- ❖ Calories: 350
- ❖ Total Fat: 14g
- ❖ Cholesterol: 95mg
- ❖ Sodium: 950mg
- ❖ Total Carbohydrates: 40g
- ❖ Dietary Fiber: 10g
- ❖ Protein: 18g
- ❖ Calcium: 35%
- ❖ Iron: 15%
- ❖ Potassium: 15%

Air Fryer Eggplant Parmesan Stacks perfectly balances hearty vegetables and indulgent cheese is an effortless recipe that results in a dish that's not just tasty but also rich in fiber and protein. Enjoy this air-fried goodness guilt-free any day of the week.

Recipe 48: Goat Cheese and Spinach Stuffed Chicken Breast

Savor the delectable flavors of this Air Fryer Goat Cheese and Spinach Stuffed Chicken Breast. This healthy and nutritious meal will make your dinner times unforgettable with its perfect blend of taste and health.

Servings: 4

Prepping Time: 15 minutes

Cook Time: 20 minutes

Difficulty: Easy

Ingredients:

- ✓ 4 boneless chicken breasts
- ✓ 1 cup spinach, chopped
- ✓ 4 ounces of goat cheese
- ✓ 1 teaspoon olive oil
- ✓ Salt and pepper to taste

- ✓ 2 teaspoons garlic powder
- ✓ 2 teaspoons onion powder

Step-by-Step Preparation:

1. Preheat your air fryer to 375°F (190°C).
2. Season the chicken breasts with salt, pepper, garlic powder, and onion powder.
3. Cut a slit into each chicken breast and stuff with spinach and goat cheese.
4. Drizzle with olive oil and place them in the air fryer.
5. Cook for 20 minutes or until the chicken is golden brown.

Nutritional Facts: (Per serving)

- ❖ Calories: 260
- ❖ Fat: 12g
- ❖ Protein: 33g
- ❖ Carbohydrates: 2g
- ❖ Fiber: 1g

Indulge in the guilt-free goodness of this Air Fryer Goat Cheese and Spinach Stuffed Chicken Breast. This easy, quick-to-prepare dish is perfect for your weekday dinner or weekend get-togethers. Experience the magic of healthy eating without compromising on taste. Enjoy!

Recipe 49: Ricotta and Spinach Stuffed Shells

Experience an effortless gourmet dining experience with our Air Fryer Ricotta and Spinach Stuffed Shells. This dish will impress with its rich flavors and elegant presentation, all without you having to spend hours in the kitchen.

Servings: 4

Prepping Time: 20 minutes

Cook Time: 15 minutes

Difficulty: Medium

Ingredients

- ✓ 16 jumbo pasta shells
- ✓ 1 cup ricotta cheese
- ✓ 2 cups fresh spinach
- ✓ 1 cup shredded mozzarella cheese
- ✓ 2 cups marinara sauce
- ✓ Salt and pepper to taste

- ✓ Fresh basil for garnish

Step-by-Step Preparation

1. Cook the pasta shells according to package instructions, then drain and let cool.
2. Wilt the spinach in a pan over medium heat while the pasta cooks.
3. Mix the ricotta, wilted spinach, half of the mozzarella, salt, and pepper in a bowl.
4. Stuff each shell with the ricotta-spinach mixture and arrange them in the air fryer basket.
5. Top the shells with marinara sauce and the remaining mozzarella.
6. Cook in the air fryer at 375°F for about 15 minutes or until the cheese is melted and bubbly.
7. Garnish with fresh basil before serving.

Nutritional Facts: (Per Serving)

- ❖ Calories: 465
- ❖ Total Fat: 18g
- ❖ Sodium: 876mg
- ❖ Total Carbs: 51g
- ❖ Dietary Fiber: 3g
- ❖ Protein: 24g

Our Air Fryer Ricotta and Spinach Stuffed Shells blend the creamy richness of ricotta, the earthy essence of spinach, and the savory allure of marinara sauce, all encased in a tender pasta shell. It's a meal that brings sophistication to your table with the simple touch of an air fryer button.

Recipe 50: Air Fried Halloumi Bites

Indulge in the savory delight of Air Fried Halloumi Bites. This crispy, golden morsels pack a delectable combination of the chewy and crunchy exterior - a perfect blend of textures that complements halloumi cheese's distinctive, tangy taste.

Servings: 4

Prepping Time: 10 minutes

Cook Time: 10 minutes

Difficulty: Easy

Ingredients

- ✓ 200g Halloumi Cheese
- ✓ 1/2 cup flour
- ✓ 1 egg, beaten
- ✓ 1 cup panko breadcrumbs
- ✓ Olive oil spray

Step-by-Step Preparation

1. Cut the halloumi into bite-sized pieces.
2. Dredge the halloumi pieces in flour, then dip them in the beaten egg, followed by the panko breadcrumbs.
3. Preheat your air fryer to 200°C/390°F.
4. Arrange the breaded halloumi in the air fryer basket and spray it with olive oil.
5. Cook for 10 minutes or until golden brown, turning halfway through cooking.

Nutritional Facts: (Per serving)

- ❖ Calories: 250
- ❖ Protein: 14g
- ❖ Carbs: 16g
- ❖ Fat: 14g
- ❖ Sodium: 730mg

This Air Fried Halloumi Bites recipe is a treat for the senses, offering an appealing look, a delicious taste, and a satisfying crunch. Whether you're a fan of halloumi or new to this cheese, you'll surely enjoy its unique flavor enhanced by the air frying process. A fast, simple, and delectable dish to include in your recipe repertoire.

Chapter 6: Nutritious Nuts and Seeds

Recipe 51: Air Fryer Roasted Almonds

Savor the delightful crunch and rich flavors of Air Fryer Roasted Almonds. This nutritious snack is an easy treat, perfect for any time of the day. You're in for a real treat with a balance of natural sweetness, savory seasoning, and an enticing aroma.

Servings: 6

Prepping Time: 5 minutes

Cook Time: 10 minutes

Difficulty: Easy

Ingredients:

- ✓ 2 cups of raw almonds
- ✓ 1 tablespoon olive oil
- ✓ Salt to taste

- ✓ 1/2 teaspoon paprika (optional)

Step-by-Step Preparation:

1. Preheat your air fryer to 300°F.
2. Toss the almonds in a bowl with olive oil, salt, and paprika until evenly coated.
3. Place the almonds in the air fryer basket, evenly spreading them.
4. Cook for 10 minutes, shaking the basket halfway through.
5. Let them cool before serving.

Nutritional Facts: (Per serving)

- ❖ Calories: 210
- ❖ Protein: 8g
- ❖ Fat: 18g
- ❖ Carbohydrates: 7g
- ❖ Fiber: 4g
- ❖ Sugar: 1g

With the perfect balance of crunch and flavor, these Air Fryer Roasted Almonds make an excellent snack or garnish for your dishes. Keep them on hand for a quick, heart-healthy treat that's delicious, easy to prepare, and full of nutritional benefits.

Recipe 52: Air Fryer Spicy Cashews

Unleash the power of your air fryer to make these zesty, crunchy, and utterly addictive Air Fryer Spicy Cashews. Perfect for a healthy snack, these cashews have an irresistible spicy kick that will tantalize your taste buds.

Servings: 4

Prepping Time: 5 minutes

Cook Time: 10 minutes

Difficulty: Easy

Ingredients

- ✓ 2 cups of raw cashews
- ✓ 1 tablespoon of olive oil
- ✓ 1 teaspoon of chili powder
- ✓ 1/2 teaspoon of smoked paprika
- ✓ 1/2 teaspoon of garlic powder
- ✓ Salt to taste

Step-by-Step Preparation

1. Preheat your air fryer to 350°F (175°C).
2. Mix the cashews with olive oil, ensuring they're evenly coated.
3. Sprinkle the chili powder, smoked paprika, garlic powder, and salt over the cashews, tossing well to combine.
4. Spread the cashews evenly in the air fryer basket.
5. Air fry for 10 minutes or until golden brown, shaking the basket halfway through to ensure even cooking.

Nutritional Facts: (Per serving)

- Calories: 262 kcal
- Protein: 7g
- Fat: 21g
- Carbs: 14g
- Fiber: 2g
- Sodium: 86mg

There you have it, a simple and spicy snack that's high in protein and filled with healthy fats. These Air Fryer Spicy Cashews are delicious but also vegan and gluten-free, making them a perfect choice for everyone. They're great for parties, picnics, or just when you fancy a tasty snack.

Recipe 53: Garlic Parmesan Pumpkin Seeds

Experience autumn's warm, nutty flavor with Air Fryer Garlic Parmesan Pumpkin Seeds. These bite-sized snacks are incredibly crunchy and packed with garlicky and cheesy flavors, making them the perfect appetizer or snack for any occasion.

Servings: 6

Prepping Time: 15 minutes

Cook Time: 10 minutes

Difficulty: Easy

Ingredients

- ✓ 2 cups raw pumpkin seeds
- ✓ 1 tablespoon olive oil
- ✓ 1 tablespoon grated Parmesan cheese
- ✓ 1/2 teaspoon garlic powder
- ✓ Salt to taste

Step-by-Step Preparation

1. Rinse and pat dry pumpkin seeds.
2. Mix pumpkin seeds, olive oil, Parmesan, garlic powder, and salt in a bowl.
3. Preheat the air fryer to 180°C.
4. Spread the seasoned seeds evenly in the air fryer basket.
5. Cook for 10 minutes, stirring halfway through, until golden and crispy.
6. Let them cool before serving.

Nutritional Facts: (Per Serving)

- Calories: 170 kcal
- Protein: 9g
- Fat: 15g
- Carbohydrates: 3g
- Sodium: 90mg

These Air Fryer Garlic Parmesan Pumpkin Seeds are delightfully crispy and flavorful. They make a fantastic snack, adding a healthful crunch to your day. This recipe is simple, quick, and a great way to enjoy the essence of fall. Enjoy them as is, or add them to your salads for an extra bite!

Recipe 54: Sweet and Spicy Pecans

Elevate your snack game with this Air Fryer Sweet and Spicy Pecans recipe. This effortless recipe brings a healthy, homemade touch to your snack drawer, offering a delectable balance of sweet, spicy, and crunchy sensations.

Servings: 6

Prepping Time: 10 minutes

Cook Time: 10 minutes

Difficulty: Easy

Ingredients:

- ✓ 2 cups pecan halves
- ✓ 1/4 cup honey
- ✓ 1 tablespoon olive oil
- ✓ 1/2 teaspoon ground cinnamon
- ✓ 1/2 teaspoon chili powder
- ✓ Salt to taste

Step-by-Step Preparation:

1. Preheat the air fryer to 350°F.
2. Combine honey, olive oil, cinnamon, chili powder, and salt in a bowl.
3. Toss the pecans in the spice mixture until evenly coated.
4. Arrange the pecans in a single layer in the air fryer basket.
5. Cook for 10 minutes, shaking the basket halfway through to ensure even cooking.
6. Allow to cool before serving.

Nutritional Facts: (Per serving)

- Calories: 286
- Fat: 27g
- Carbohydrates: 12g
- Fiber: 3g
- Protein: 3g
- Sodium: 98mg

These Air Fryer Sweet and Spicy Pecans are an excellent go-to snack or can elevate your salad or dessert topping. They're a delightful blend of crunch, spice, and sweetness - all made effortlessly in your air fryer. Make a batch today and enjoy a healthier, tastier snack alternative.

Recipe 55: Chili Lime Pistachios

Experience the perfect crunch and zest with Air Fryer Chili Lime Pistachios. These flavorful nuts pack a punch with a blend of tangy lime and spicy chili, a treat that will tantalize your taste buds!

Servings: 6-8

Prepping Time: 10 minutes

Cook Time: 10 minutes

Difficulty: Easy

Ingredients:

- ✓ 2 cups raw pistachios
- ✓ Zest and juice of 2 limes
- ✓ 1 tablespoon chili powder
- ✓ 1 teaspoon sea salt
- ✓ 1 tablespoon olive oil

Step-by-Step Preparation:

1. Preheat your air fryer to 350°F (180°C).
2. Combine the pistachios, lime zest, lime juice, chili powder, sea salt, and olive oil in a bowl. Stir until all pistachios are evenly coated.
3. Transfer the coated pistachios to the air fryer basket. Cook for 10 minutes, shaking halfway through.
4. Let them cool completely before serving.

Nutritional Facts: (Per serving)

- Calories: 225
- Protein: 8g
- Fat: 18g
- Carbohydrates: 10g
- Fiber: 4g

There you have it – the perfect blend of zesty, spicy, and crunchy in one delicious bite. These Air Fryer Chili Lime Pistachios make a fabulous snack, whether hosting a party or enjoying them on a relaxing afternoon. Happy snacking!

Recipe 56: Honey Roasted Sunflower Seeds

Embrace a healthy snack with a sweet twist: Air Fryer Honey Roasted Sunflower Seeds. They're a perfect blend of crunch and sweetness, satisfying your cravings while providing essential nutrients.

Servings: 6

Prepping Time: 5 minutes

Cook Time: 15 minutes

Difficulty: Easy

Ingredients

- ✓ 2 cups raw sunflower seeds
- ✓ 3 tablespoons honey
- ✓ 1/2 teaspoon salt
- ✓ 1 tablespoon olive oil

Step-by-Step Preparation

1. Preheat the air fryer to 320°F.
2. Combine sunflower seeds, honey, salt, and olive oil in a bowl.
3. Spread the seeds evenly in the air fryer basket.
4. Air fry for 15 minutes, shaking the basket every 5 minutes for even roasting.
5. Allow to cool before serving.

Nutritional Facts: (Per serving)

- ❖ Calories: 206
- ❖ Protein: 6g
- ❖ Fat: 18g
- ❖ Carbohydrates: 9g
- ❖ Fiber: 3g

Air Fryer Honey Roasted Sunflower Seeds are an easy-to-make snack and a delightful way to infuse nutrition into your diet. Whether you enjoy them by the handful or as a crunchy topping, these sweet and savory seeds will surely be a hit!

Recipe 57: Spiced Sesame Seed Mix

Spiced Sesame Seed Mix is an excellent choice for a healthy, flavorful snack. Perfectly roasted in an air fryer, these seeds bring a fusion of spices that will leave your tastebuds craving more. Ideal for topping salads, yogurts, or just munching on the go!

Servings: 4

Prepping Time: 10 minutes

Cook Time: 10 minutes

Difficulty: Easy

Ingredients:

- ✓ 1 cup Sesame Seeds
- ✓ 1/2 teaspoon Cayenne Pepper
- ✓ 1 teaspoon Turmeric Powder
- ✓ 1/2 teaspoon Salt
- ✓ 1 teaspoon Olive Oil

Step-by-Step Preparation:

1. Mix sesame seeds, cayenne pepper, turmeric, and salt in a bowl.
2. Drizzle olive oil over the mixture and toss until the seeds are evenly coated.
3. Preheat the air fryer to 180°C (350°F).
4. Spread the seed mix in the air fryer basket and roast for 10 minutes, shaking midway to ensure even roasting.
5. Allow the mix to cool before consuming.

Nutritional Facts: (Per serving)

- Calories: 206
- Protein: 6.4g
- Carbohydrates: 7.3g
- Fat: 18g
- Sodium: 294mg
- Fiber: 3.4g

The Air Fryer Spiced, Sesame Seed Mix, is a versatile, tasty, and healthy choice that is quick to prepare. Whether you want a snack for a party or something different for your daily munching, this recipe will surely delight your palate and impress your guests. Make your snack time healthier and more exciting with this incredible mix!

Recipe 58: Air Fried Walnuts with Rosemary

Indulge in these flavorful and heart-healthy Air Fried Walnuts with Rosemary, a perfect snack to crunch anytime. It's an effortless recipe with a distinctive aroma that pairs perfectly with your favorite beverage or as a salad topping.

Servings: 4

Prepping Time: 5 minutes

Cook Time: 10 minutes

Difficulty: Easy

Ingredients:

- ✓ 2 cups of raw walnuts
- ✓ 1 tablespoon olive oil
- ✓ 2 tablespoons fresh rosemary, finely chopped
- ✓ Salt to taste

Step-by-Step Preparation:

1. Preheat the air fryer to 350°F (175°C).
2. Combine walnuts, olive oil, chopped rosemary, and salt in a bowl. Toss until walnuts are well coated.
3. Place the coated walnuts in the air fryer basket, spreading them in a single layer.
4. Air fry for 10 minutes or until they're golden brown and fragrant. Shake the basket halfway through to ensure even roasting.
5. Allow to cool before serving.

Nutritional Facts: (Per serving)

- ❖ Calories: 345
- ❖ Protein: 7.8g
- ❖ Carbohydrates: 6.1g
- ❖ Fat: 34.3g
- ❖ Fiber: 3.9g
- ❖ Sodium: 2mg
- ❖ Protein: 6.4g

Enjoy these crispy, nutritious, and flavorful Air Fried Walnuts with Rosemary. Whether as a healthy snack during your busy day or a complement to your meal, these walnuts, with their earthy aroma and delightful crunch, will surely add an extra zest to your culinary adventures.

Recipe 59: Air Fryer Crunchy Peanut Butter Granola

Dive into the world of healthy snacks with this Air Fryer Crunchy Peanut Butter Granola. This simple yet delicious recipe combines wholesome ingredients to create a crisp, sweet, nutty granola. Perfect for breakfast or as a snack!

Servings: 6

Prepping Time: 10 minutes

Cook Time: 20 minutes

Difficulty: Easy

Ingredients:

- ✓ 2 cups rolled oats
- ✓ 1 cup natural peanut butter
- ✓ 1/2 cup honey
- ✓ 1/2 cup mixed nuts, chopped
- ✓ 1/2 cup dried fruit, optional

Step-by-Step Preparation:

1. Preheat the air fryer to 350°F (175°C).
2. Combine oats, peanut butter, and honey in a bowl. Mix until oats are thoroughly coated.
3. Spread the mixture evenly in the air fryer basket.
4. Air fry for 10 minutes, shake, then fry for another 10 minutes until golden brown.
5. Remove granola from the air fryer, and mix in chopped nuts and dried fruit. Allow to cool before serving.

Nutritional Facts: (Per serving)

- Calories: 415
- Protein: 18g
- Fat: 24g
- Carbohydrates: 44g
- Fiber: 6g
- Sugar: 16g

This Air Fryer Crunchy Peanut Butter Granola is a delight for the taste buds! Not only is it a nutritious and filling breakfast option, but it also serves as a fantastic topping for yogurt or a snack on the go. Try this easy and delightful recipe; you won't be disappointed!

Recipe 60: Cinnamon and Sugar Coated Almonds

Enjoy a crispy, flavorful treat with these Air Fryer Cinnamon and Sugar Coated Almonds. A perfect combination of health and taste, these snackable delights will leave you wanting more.

Servings: 4

Prepping Time: 10 minutes

Cook Time: 10 minutes

Difficulty: Easy

Ingredients:

- ✓ 2 cups raw almonds
- ✓ 1 tablespoon cinnamon
- ✓ 1/2 cup sugar
- ✓ 1 egg white
- ✓ 1 teaspoon vanilla extract

Step-by-Step Preparation:

1. Preheat your air fryer to 300°F.
2. Whisk the egg white and vanilla extract until frothy in a bowl.
3. Add almonds to the mixture, ensuring they are well coated.
4. In a separate bowl, mix sugar and cinnamon, then add the almonds, tossing them until fully covered.
5. Arrange the almonds in the air fryer basket in a single layer.
6. Cook for 10 minutes, shaking the basket halfway through to ensure even cooking.

Nutritional Facts: (Per Serving)

- Calories: 320
- Protein: 12g
- Fat: 24g
- Carbohydrates: 18g
- Sugar: 10g

These Air Fryer Cinnamon and Sugar Coated Almonds are perfect for indulging, healthy snacks. They're irresistibly crunchy and flavorful, so make a batch and enjoy the perfect balance of sweetness and spice in every bite!

Chapter 7: Protein Snacks and Starters

Recipe 61: Air Fryer Cheese and Bacon Rolls

Dive into the world of finger-licking snacks with our Air Fryer Cheese and Bacon Rolls. A perfect combination of crispiness, cheesiness, and a burst of flavors, these rolls are the ultimate treat to satisfy your snack cravings.

Servings: 4

Prepping Time: 15 minutes

Cook Time: 10 minutes

Difficulty: Easy

Ingredients:

- ✓ 4 strips of bacon
- ✓ 1 cup shredded cheddar cheese
- ✓ 8 egg roll wrappers
- ✓ Cooking spray

Step-by-Step Preparation:

1. Preheat your air fryer to 400 degrees.
2. Cook the bacon until crisp, then crumble it.
3. Mix the crumbled bacon and shredded cheese.
4. Divide the mixture evenly among the egg roll wrappers, roll them tightly, and seal the edges with water.
5. Spray the rolls with cooking spray and place them in the air fryer.
6. Cook for 10 minutes or until golden brown.

Nutritional Facts: (Per Serving)

- Calories: 280 kcal
- Protein: 12g
- Fat: 17g
- Carbohydrates: 20g
- Sodium: 580mg
- Fiber: 1g
- Sugar: 1g

These easy-to-make Air Fryer Cheese and Bacon Rolls will be a hit at your next gathering. The perfect blend of crunchy bacon and melted cheese in a crispy roll is irresistible. Keep your taste buds wanting more with this fantastic snack!

Recipe 62: Crunchy Zucchini Fries

Savor the goodness of garden-fresh zucchini with these Air Fryer Crunchy Zucchini Fries. These are perfect as a healthy snack or appetizer, boasting a crisp, golden exterior surrounding a tender zucchini interior, all without the guilt of deep frying.

Servings: 4

Prepping Time: 10 minutes

Cook Time: 10 minutes

Difficulty: Easy

Ingredients:

- ✓ 2 medium zucchinis
- ✓ 1/2 cup all-purpose flour
- ✓ 2 eggs, beaten
- ✓ 1 cup panko breadcrumbs
- ✓ 1/2 cup parmesan cheese, grated
- ✓ Salt and pepper to taste

- ✓ Cooking spray

Step-by-Step Preparation:

1. Cut zucchini into fries-like sticks. Set aside.
2. Place the flour, beaten eggs, and a mixture of panko, parmesan, salt, and pepper in separate bowls.
3. Dredge zucchini fries in flour, dip them into the eggs, and coat them with panko.
4. Arrange the zucchini fries in the air fryer basket. Lightly spray with cooking spray.
5. Cook at 400°F for 10 minutes or until golden brown and crispy. Serve immediately.

Nutritional Facts: (Per Serving)

- ❖ Calories: 180
- ❖ Fat: 4.5g
- ❖ Saturated Fat: 1.5g
- ❖ Cholesterol: 65mg
- ❖ Sodium: 200mg
- ❖ Carbohydrates: 27g
- ❖ Fiber: 2g
- ❖ Sugar: 4g
- ❖ Protein: 9g

Air Fryer Crunchy Zucchini Fries offer a delightful combination of health and indulgence, creating a snack you can enjoy anytime. They're simple to prepare and showcase the air fryer's capabilities to transform everyday ingredients into delectable treats. Serve with your favorite dip for an added touch of taste. Enjoy!

Recipe 63: Air Fryer Protein Packed Quesadilla

Packed with protein and deliciously cheesy, these Air Fryer Protein Packed Quesadillas are perfect for a quick, healthy meal. They're crispy, flavorful, and easy to whip up in the Air Fryer!

Servings: 4

Prepping Time: 15 minutes

Cook Time: 10 minutes

Difficulty: Easy

Ingredients:

- ✓ 4 large whole-grain tortillas
- ✓ 1 cup of cooked chicken, diced
- ✓ 1 can of black beans, drained and rinsed
- ✓ 1 cup of shredded cheese (cheddar, Monterey Jack, or a mix)
- ✓ 1/2 cup of Greek yogurt
- ✓ 1/4 cup of salsa

- ✓ Cooking spray

Step-by-Step Preparation:

1. Spread Greek yogurt on one-half of each tortilla.
2. Top with chicken, black beans, and cheese.
3. Fold the tortilla in half, and press gently.
4. Spray each side of the quesadilla lightly with cooking spray.
5. Place the quesadillas in the Air Fryer basket.
6. Cook at 375°F for 5 minutes, flip, then cook for another 5 minutes or until crispy and golden.
7. Serve hot with salsa.

Nutritional Facts: (Per Serving)

- ❖ Calories: 395
- ❖ Protein: 32g
- ❖ Carbohydrates: 35g
- ❖ Fat: 13g
- ❖ Fiber: 6g
- ❖ Sodium: 735mg

Enjoy these Air Fryer Protein Packed Quesadillas as a fulfilling meal. They're great for dinner or a snack on the go. Perfectly crispy and golden on the outside, loaded with nourishing ingredients on the inside – a fantastic way to combine taste and health in one delightful dish!

Recipe 64: Jalapeno Poppers with Cream Cheese and Bacon

Enjoy a bite of spicy crunch with our Air Fryer Jalapeno Poppers. These poppers are the perfect finger food for any gathering. Ready in minutes, they're an exciting and healthier alternative to deep frying.

Servings: 4-6

Prepping Time: 15 minutes

Cook Time: 10 minutes

Difficulty: Easy

Ingredients:

- ✓ 12 jalapenos
- ✓ 8 oz cream cheese, softened
- ✓ 1 cup shredded cheddar cheese
- ✓ 6 slices bacon, cooked and crumbled
- ✓ 1/2 cup bread crumbs

- ✓ Salt and pepper to taste

Step-by-Step Preparation:

1. Preheat your air fryer to 375°F (190°C).
2. Cut jalapenos in half lengthwise and scoop out seeds and membranes.
3. Mix a bowl of cream cheese, cheddar cheese, bacon, salt, and pepper.
4. Stuff each jalapeno half with the cheese mixture, then roll in bread crumbs.
5. Arrange stuffed jalapenos in the air fryer basket.
6. Cook for 10 minutes or until golden and crispy.
7. Allow to cool slightly before serving.

Nutritional Facts per serving:

- ❖ Calories: 210
- ❖ Fat: 16g
- ❖ Carbohydrates: 6g
- ❖ Protein: 11g

These Air Fryer Jalapeno Poppers are an irresistible treat, offering a creamy, crispy, and spicy balance. Ideal for parties, picnics, or a delicious snack at home. The air fryer delivers all the crunch without excess oil, making them a healthier choice that doesn't compromise flavor.

Recipe 65: Buffalo Cauliflower Bites

These delicious Air Fryer Buffalo Cauliflower Bites are a game-changing, plant-based treat. They combine the tangy heat of buffalo sauce with cauliflower's natural sweetness, providing a healthier alternative to traditional game-day snacks.

Servings: 4

Prepping Time: 15 minutes

Cook Time: 15 minutes

Difficulty: Easy

Ingredients:

- 1 head of cauliflower, cut into florets
- 1 cup of buffalo sauce
- 1 tbsp of olive oil
- 1 tsp of garlic powder
- 1/2 tsp of salt
- 1/2 tsp of pepper

- ✓ Blue cheese or ranch dressing (optional)
- ✓ Fresh parsley for garnish (optional)

Step-by-Step Preparation:

1. Preheat your air fryer to 375°F (190°C).
2. In a large bowl, toss the cauliflower florets with olive oil, garlic powder, salt, and pepper.
3. Transfer the cauliflower to the air fryer basket, spreading it out evenly.
4. Air fry for 12-15 minutes or until the cauliflower is golden and crispy.
5. While the cauliflower is hot, toss it in the buffalo sauce until it is well-coated.
6. Serve the cauliflower bites hot, optionally with blue cheese or ranch dressing, and garnish with fresh parsley.

Nutritional Facts per serving:

- ❖ Calories 104
- ❖ Fat 3.4g
- ❖ Sodium 1250mg
- ❖ Carbs 16g
- ❖ Fiber 6g
- ❖ Sugar 6g
- ❖ Protein 4g

Air Fryer Buffalo Cauliflower Bites are a fantastic, guilt-free choice for those looking to enjoy a flavorful snack without straying from their health-conscious goals. Crunchy, spicy, and utterly addictive, they will surely be a crowd-pleaser at your next gathering. Say goodbye to greasy game-day fare and hello to this delightful veggie dish!

Recipe 66: Cheesy Spinach and Artichoke Dip

Delve into the world of delightful appetizers with this Air Fryer Cheesy Spinach and Artichoke Dip, a delightful mix of fresh veggies, cream cheese, and a hint of spice. This dish, rich in flavors, perfectly combines creamy texture and cheesy goodness.

Servings: 6

Prepping Time: 10

Minutes Cook Time: 20

Minutes Difficulty: Easy

Ingredients:

- 2 cups Fresh Spinach
- 1 cup Chopped Artichoke Hearts
- 1 cup Cream Cheese
- 1 cup Grated Mozzarella Cheese
- 1/2 cup Grated Parmesan Cheese
- 2 Garlic Cloves, minced

- ✓ 1/2 teaspoon Red Pepper Flakes
- ✓ Salt and Pepper to taste

Step-by-Step Preparation:

1. Combine spinach, artichokes, cream cheese, mozzarella, parmesan, garlic, red pepper flakes, salt, and Pepper in a bowl.
2. Preheat the air fryer to 375°F (190°C).
3. Transfer the mixture to an air fryer-safe dish and spread evenly.
4. Cook for 20 minutes until the top is golden and bubbly.
5. Serve warm with your favorite chips or crusty bread.

Nutritional Facts per serving:

- ❖ Calories: 250
- ❖ Fat: 18g
- ❖ Sodium: 520mg
- ❖ Carbohydrates: 6g
- ❖ Fiber: 1g
- ❖ Protein: 10g

This Air Fryer Cheesy Spinach and Artichoke Dip is a surefire hit at your next gathering, featuring fresh ingredients, a creamy texture, and loads of cheesy goodness. Its simple preparation, and unique cooking method will make your kitchen the heart of any party.

Recipe 67: Air Fryer Mini Sliders

Unveil the delectable taste of homemade Air Fryer Mini Sliders. The perfect finger food for any gathering, these sliders deliver bite-sized bursts of classic burger flavors in a healthier air-fried version.

Servings: 8

Prepping Time: 15 minutes

Cook Time: 10 minutes

Difficulty: Easy

Ingredients:

- ✓ 1 lb lean ground beef
- ✓ 8 mini buns
- ✓ 1 small onion, chopped
- ✓ 1/2 cup shredded cheddar cheese
- ✓ Lettuce and tomato for garnish
- ✓ Salt and pepper to taste

Step-by-Step Preparation:

1. Preheat your air fryer to 375°F.
2. Mix ground beef, onion, salt, and pepper in a bowl.
3. Shape the mixture into 8 small patties.
4. Place the patties in the air fryer and cook for 10 minutes, flipping halfway through.
5. Add cheese to the patties at the last minute to melt.
6. Assemble the sliders with mini buns, patties, lettuce, and tomato.

Nutritional Facts per serving:

- Calories: 200
- Fat: 9g
- Protein: 16g
- Carbohydrates: 15g
- Fiber: 1g
- Sugar: 3g

Enjoy these savory Air Fryer Mini Sliders. They're crispy on the outside, juicy on the inside, and layered with fresh veggies. A healthier twist on a classic favorite, they're sure to be a hit at your next family dinner or backyard barbeque.

Recipe 68: Chicken Satay Skewers with Peanut Sauce

A staple of Southeast Asian cuisine, these Air Fryer Chicken Satay Skewers with Peanut Sauce offer a delicious meal. Perfect for a midweek dinner or a party appetizer, they're easy to make and always a crowd-pleaser.

Servings: 4

Prepping Time: 15 minutes

Cook Time: 10 minutes

Difficulty: Easy

Ingredients:

- ✓ 500g chicken breast, cut into thin strips
- ✓ 1 tablespoon soy sauce
- ✓ 2 tablespoons honey
- ✓ 2 tablespoons curry powder
- ✓ Salt and pepper to taste

- ✓ 8 wooden skewers, soaked in water for 30 mins
- ✓ 1/2 cup creamy peanut butter
- ✓ 2 tablespoons rice vinegar
- ✓ 1 tablespoon lime juice
- ✓ 2 tablespoons water
- ✓ 1 tablespoon brown sugar
- ✓ Crushed peanuts and fresh cilantro for garnish

Step-by-Step Preparation:

1. Marinate chicken strips with soy sauce, honey, curry powder, salt, and pepper. Let it rest for at least 15 minutes.
2. Thread the chicken onto the soaked skewers.
3. Preheat the air fryer to 400°F (200°C). Cook the skewers for 10 minutes or until the chicken is thoroughly cooked.
4. Combine peanut butter, rice vinegar, lime juice, water, and brown sugar in a bowl for the peanut sauce. Mix until smooth.
5. Serve the chicken skewers with the peanut sauce. Garnish with crushed peanuts and fresh cilantro.

Nutritional Facts per Serving:

- ❖ Calories: 385
- ❖ Fat: 18g
- ❖ Carbohydrates: 16g
- ❖ Protein: 42g

Perfectly cooked and brimming with flavors, these Air Fryer Chicken Satay Skewers with Peanut Sauce will transport your tastebuds to Southeast Asia. Convenient to cook and irresistibly tasty, this dish is a fabulous choice for those seeking a healthier yet flavorful option. Enjoy your homemade Chicken Satay!

Recipe 69: Spiced Chickpea Popcorn

Ready for a healthy snack with a crunchy bite and full of flavor? Try this Air Fryer Spiced Chickpea Popcorn recipe. It's an excellent option for munching during movie nights or casual gatherings and a delightful alternative to traditional popcorn.

Servings: 4-6

Prepping Time: 10 minutes

Cook Time: 20 minutes

Difficulty: Easy

Ingredients:

1. 2 cans of chickpeas (15 oz each)
2. 1 tbsp olive oil
3. 1 tsp smoked paprika
4. 1/2 tsp cayenne pepper
5. Salt to taste
6. Freshly ground black pepper to taste

Step-by-Step Preparation:

1. Rinse and thoroughly dry the chickpeas.
2. Toss chickpeas with olive oil, paprika, cayenne, salt, and black pepper.
3. Place chickpeas in the air fryer basket.
4. Cook at 375°F (190°C) for 20 minutes, shaking halfway through to ensure even cooking.
5. Let them cool for a few minutes before serving.

Nutritional Facts per Serving:

- ❖ Calories: 150 kcal
- ❖ Protein: 6 g
- ❖ Carbohydrates: 25 g
- ❖ Fiber: 5 g
- ❖ Fat: 3 g

Now that you've mastered Air Fryer Spiced Chickpea Popcorn, you've unlocked a versatile snack tailored to any palate. Experiment with different seasonings to create your perfect blend. Enjoy this wholesome and flavorful treat that adds a unique twist to your snack time.

Recipe 70: Cheesy Pepperoni Protein Pizza Rolls

Experience the cheesy, meaty delight of Air Fryer Cheesy Pepperoni Protein Pizza Rolls. Packed with flavor, they make a perfect appetizer or snack that is sure to impress everyone at your next gathering.

Servings: 4

Prepping Time: 10 minutes

Cook Time: 15 minutes

Difficulty: Easy

Ingredients:

- ✓ 8 whole-grain tortillas
- ✓ 1 cup of low-fat mozzarella cheese
- ✓ 16 pepperoni slices
- ✓ 1/2 cup pizza sauce
- ✓ 1/4 cup grated Parmesan cheese

- ✓ 1 tablespoon Italian seasoning
- ✓ Cooking spray

Step-by-Step Preparation:

1. Preheat your air fryer to 390°F.
2. Lay out tortillas, spread pizza sauce evenly on each, sprinkle mozzarella cheese, and place 2 pepperoni slices per tortilla.
3. Roll each tortilla tightly, then secure it with a toothpick.
4. Spray each roll with cooking spray, and sprinkle with Parmesan cheese and Italian seasoning.
5. Arrange rolls in the air fryer basket. Cook for 10-15 minutes or until golden brown.
6. Let cool before serving, then enjoy with your favorite dipping sauce.

Nutritional Facts: (Per serving)

- ❖ Calories: 200
- ❖ Protein: 14g
- ❖ Carbohydrates: 20g
- ❖ Fat: 8g
- ❖ Sodium: 500mg

These Air Fryer Cheesy Pepperoni Protein Pizza Rolls are a must-try. They're tasty and loaded with protein, making them an excellent choice for health-conscious individuals. Savor the flavorful bite of this appetizer, and be amazed at how fast they disappear from the serving plate!

Chapter 8: Power Breakfast Recipes

Recipe 71: Protein-Packed French Toast Sticks

Indulge in the heavenly delight of Air Fryer Protein Packed French Toast Sticks. These crispy, flavorful sticks are perfect for a quick breakfast or a healthy snack, delivering a protein punch that'll keep you energized all day.

Servings: 4

Prepping Time: 10 minutes

Cook Time: 10 minutes

Difficulty: Easy

Ingredients:

- ✓ 8 slices whole grain bread
- ✓ 4 large eggs
- ✓ 1 cup milk (dairy or plant-based)
- ✓ 1 scoop protein powder

- ✓ 1 tsp vanilla extract
- ✓ Cinnamon to taste
- ✓ Syrup for dipping

Step-by-Step Preparation:

1. Cut each bread slice into four sticks.
2. Mix eggs, milk, protein powder, vanilla extract, and cinnamon in a bowl.
3. Dip each breadstick into the mixture, ensuring it's fully coated.
4. Arrange sticks in the air fryer basket, leaving some space between them.
5. Air fry at 375°F for 10 minutes, flipping halfway through.
6. Serve hot with syrup.

Nutritional Facts: (Per serving)

- ❖ Calories: 300
- ❖ Protein: 20g
- ❖ Carbs: 40g
- ❖ Fat: 10g

Relish the sweet indulgence of these Air Fryer Protein Packed French Toast Sticks. They offer a healthy, satisfying twist on the classic French toast, making them the perfect recipe for those striving for a protein-rich diet without compromising taste.

Recipe 72: Ham and Egg Breakfast Burritos

Start your day with these delicious Air Fryer Ham and Egg Breakfast Burritos. Easy to make, packed with protein, and wonderfully crispy, they are the perfect grab-and-go breakfast for a busy morning.

Servings: 4

Prepping Time: 15 minutes

Cook Time: 10 minutes

Difficulty: Easy

Ingredients:

- ✓ 4 large flour tortillas
- ✓ 4 eggs
- ✓ 1 cup of diced ham
- ✓ 1 cup of shredded cheddar cheese
- ✓ 1/4 cup of chopped green onions
- ✓ Salt and pepper to taste

Step-by-Step Preparation:

1. Scramble the eggs in a non-stick pan over medium heat.
2. Add the diced ham and cook until the eggs are done.
3. Lay the tortillas and evenly distribute the scrambled eggs, ham, cheese, and chopped green onions.
4. Roll up the burritos and place them in the air fryer.
5. Cook at 360°F for 10 minutes until the burritos are golden and crispy.
6. Allow to cool for a couple of minutes before serving.

Nutritional Facts: (Per serving)

- Calories: 365
- Fat: 18g
- Protein: 21g
- Carbohydrates: 27g
- Fiber: 2g
- Sugar: 3g

These Air Fryer Ham and Egg Breakfast Burritos are a delicious, quick, and convenient breakfast option. Whether you're on the run or want a flavorful start to your day, these burritos will surely hit the spot!

Recipe 73: Breakfast Sausage Links

Savor the delight of a wholesome breakfast with our Air Fryer Breakfast Sausage Links recipe. These juicy, crispy, and perfectly cooked sausages will make your morning meal special. It's a hassle-free recipe that can turn an ordinary morning into a festive feast.

Servings: 4

Prepping Time: 10 minutes

Cook Time: 10-12 minutes

Difficulty: Easy

Ingredients:

- ✓ 1 pound of breakfast sausage links
- ✓ Cooking spray
- ✓ Your preferred spices or herbs for flavor (optional)

Step-by-Step Preparation:

1. Preheat the air fryer to 400°F (200°C) for 5 minutes.
2. Lightly spray the sausages with the cooking spray.
3. Arrange the sausages in a single layer in the air fryer basket, ensuring they don't overlap.
4. Cook for 5-6 minutes, then flip the sausages.
5. Continue cooking for another 5-6 minutes until browned and cooked.
6. Sprinkle with your preferred spices or herbs, if desired.
7. Serve hot with your choice of side.

Nutritional Facts: (Per serving)

- Calories: 250
- Protein: 13g
- Carbohydrates: 1g
- Fat: 20g
- Saturated Fat: 7g
- Cholesterol: 60mg
- Sodium: 590mg
- Sugar: 0g

Air Fryer Breakfast Sausage Links make for a delectable, protein-packed breakfast to kick-start your day. Quick, easy, and tantalizingly tasty, this recipe is perfect for those busy mornings. Enjoy these air-fried sausages or pair them the eggs, toast, or pancakes for a complete meal. Add this delightful treat to your breakfast routine today!

Recipe 74: Bacon and Cheese Muffins

Kickstart your day with these delightful Air Fryer Bacon and Cheese Muffins. Crispy bacon, melty cheese, and a fluffy muffin base make this recipe an absolute winner for breakfast or brunch, with a unique air-fryer twist that keeps them light and guilt-free.

Servings: 6

Prepping Time: 15 minutes

Cook Time: 20 minutes

Difficulty: Easy

Ingredients:

- 1 cup all-purpose flour
- 1 tsp baking powder
- 1/2 tsp salt
- 2 eggs
- 1/2 cup milk
- 1/4 cup vegetable oil

- ✓ 1/2 cup shredded cheese
- ✓ 4 bacon strips, cooked and crumbled

Step-by-Step Preparation:

1. Combine the flour, baking powder, and salt in a bowl.
2. In another bowl, beat eggs, milk, and oil until smooth. Stir this into the dry ingredients.
3. Fold in the shredded cheese and bacon.
4. Divide the mixture among six greased muffin cups.
5. Preheat the air fryer to 350°F. Bake the muffins in the air fryer for 20 minutes or until a toothpick comes out clean.

Nutritional Facts: (Per Serving)

- ❖ Calories: 232
- ❖ Fat: 14g
- ❖ Carbohydrates: 17g
- ❖ Protein: 8g
- ❖ Sugar: 2g
- ❖ Sodium: 425mg

These scrumptious Air Fryer Bacon and Cheese Muffins are the perfect mix of savory and cheesy flavors. Enjoy them fresh out of the fryer for the ultimate breakfast treat, or pack them for a wholesome snack on the go. These muffins will become your new breakfast favorite quick, easy, and oh-so-tasty!

Recipe 75: Spinach and Feta Egg White Wraps

Begin your day with a healthy twist - Air Fryer Spinach and Feta Egg White Wraps. These nutritious and satisfying wraps are packed with protein and fiber, making them an ideal breakfast choice for fitness enthusiasts.

Servings: 4

Prepping Time: 15 minutes

Cook Time: 10 minutes

Difficulty: Easy

Ingredients:

- 8 egg whites
- 2 cups fresh spinach
- 1/2 cup crumbled feta cheese
- 4 whole-grain tortilla wraps
- Salt and pepper to taste
- Non-stick cooking spray

Step-by-Step Preparation:

1. Beat the egg whites with salt and pepper.
2. Spray the air fryer basket with non-stick cooking spray.
3. Pour the beaten egg whites into the basket and cook at 300°F for 10 minutes or until firm.
4. While the eggs are cooking, steam the spinach until wilted.
5. Divide the cooked egg whites and spinach evenly among the tortillas.
6. Sprinkle with feta cheese.
7. Roll each tortilla tightly, slice in half, and serve.

Nutritional Facts: (Per Serving)

- Calories: 280
- Protein: 20g
- Fat: 8g
- Carbohydrates: 28g
- Fiber: 4g
- Sodium: 570mg

These Air Fryer Spinach and Feta Egg White Wraps are delicious and loaded with nutrients to fuel your day. Quick and easy to prepare, they make a perfect go-to meal for those busy mornings or post-workout refreshments. Enjoy the burst of flavor and health in every bite!

Recipe 76: Turkey Sausage Patties

Start your day with an enticing breakfast featuring these tasty Air Fryer Turkey Sausage Patties. They're succulent, filled with spices, and unbelievably easy to whip up, providing a healthier alternative to traditional sausage patties.

Servings: 4

Prepping Time: 10 minutes

Cook Time: 12 minutes

Difficulty: Easy

Ingredients:

- ✓ 1 lb ground turkey
- ✓ 1 tsp dried sage
- ✓ 1/2 tsp salt
- ✓ 1/2 tsp black pepper
- ✓ 1/4 tsp dried thyme
- ✓ 1/4 tsp crushed red pepper flakes

- ✓ 1/4 tsp ground nutmeg
- ✓ Olive oil spray

Step-by-Step Preparation:

1. Mix the ground turkey with sage, salt, pepper, thyme, red pepper flakes, and nutmeg in a large bowl.
2. Shape the mixture into four equal-sized patties.
3. Spray the air fryer basket with olive oil and place the patties.
4. Air fry at 375°F for 6 minutes on each side until fully cooked and golden brown.

Nutritional Facts: (Per serving)

- ❖ Calories: 167
- ❖ Protein: 22g
- ❖ Carbs: 0g
- ❖ Fat: 8g
- ❖ Sodium: 453mg

With these Air Fryer Turkey Sausage Patties, you've got a nutritious, protein-packed breakfast that is as delicious as it is simple to prepare. Serve them with your favorite side, eggs, toast, or pancakes, and make your mornings extra special.

Recipe 77: Sweet Potato and Black Bean Breakfast Burritos

Start your day on a healthy, delicious note with these Air Fryer Sweet Potato and Black Bean Breakfast Burritos. This simple, wholesome recipe ensures a burst of flavors packed with nutrients. It's the perfect blend of sweet, savory, and spicy to kickstart your morning!

Servings: 4

Prepping Time: 20 minutes

Cook Time: 15 minutes

Difficulty: Medium

Ingredients

- ✓ 2 large sweet potatoes, peeled and diced
- ✓ 1 cup black beans, rinsed and drained
- ✓ 1 small onion, chopped
- ✓ 2 cloves garlic, minced
- ✓ 4 large tortillas

- ✓ 1 cup shredded cheese
- ✓ Salt and pepper to taste
- ✓ 1 tablespoon olive oil
- ✓ Fresh cilantro and lime for garnish

Step-by-Step Preparation

1. Toss sweet potatoes with olive oil, salt, and pepper and air fry at 400F for 10-15 minutes until tender.
2. In a pan, sauté onions, and garlic until fragrant. Add black beans, cooked sweet potatoes, and cook for a few more minutes.
3. Lay the tortillas and evenly distribute the sweet potato and black bean mixture. Sprinkle cheese on top.
4. Roll up the tortillas and place them in the air fryer for about 3-5 minutes or until crispy and golden brown.
5. Cut the burritos in half and serve with fresh cilantro and a squeeze of lime.

Nutritional Facts: (Per serving)

- ❖ Calories: 420
- ❖ Protein: 15g
- ❖ Carbs: 68g
- ❖ Fat: 12g
- ❖ Fiber: 11g
- ❖ Sugar: 8g

Enjoy a fulfilling breakfast with these Air Fryer Sweet Potato and Black Bean Breakfast Burritos. These burritos provide the ideal start to your day. Make them ahead of time for a quick grab-and-go breakfast, or serve them fresh for a delightful weekend brunch!

Recipe 78: Greek Yogurt Pancakes

Savor a morning delight with this fluffy and light Air Fryer Greek Yogurt Pancakes recipe. These pancakes are a healthy alternative to start your day.

Servings: 4

Prepping Time: 15 minutes

Cook Time: 10 minutes

Difficulty: Easy

Ingredients:

- ✓ 1 cup Greek yogurt
- ✓ 2 large eggs
- ✓ 1 cup whole wheat flour
- ✓ 2 tsp baking powder
- ✓ 1 tsp vanilla extract
- ✓ A pinch of salt
- ✓ Maple syrup for serving

- ✓ Fresh berries for garnish

Step-by-Step Preparation:

1. In a large bowl, mix Greek yogurt and eggs until smooth.
2. Add flour, baking powder, vanilla extract, and salt. Mix until combined.
3. Preheat your air fryer to 350°F (175°C).
4. Spoon 1/4 cup of batter per pancake onto the air fryer basket, ensuring enough space between each.
5. Cook for 5 minutes or until golden brown, then flip and cook for another 2-3 minutes.
6. Serve hot with a drizzle of maple syrup and garnish with fresh berries.

Nutritional Facts: (Per serving)

- ❖ Calories: 200
- ❖ Protein: 12g
- ❖ Carbohydrates: 28g
- ❖ Fat: 5g
- ❖ Fiber: 4g
- ❖ Sugar: 5g

These Air Fryer Greek Yogurt Pancakes will bring a smile to your face and a healthy kick to your breakfast routine. The air fryer gives them a perfect, even cook while keeping them light and fluffy. Enjoy them guilt-free any day of the week.

Recipe 79: Bacon, Egg, and Cheese Biscuits

Dive into a delightful breakfast with Air Fryer Bacon, Egg, and Cheese Biscuits. These hearty, homemade biscuits with crispy bacon, creamy melted cheese, and fluffy scrambled eggs are the perfect way to start your day. Using the air fryer makes these breakfast goodies extra crispy and gives them a wonderful golden-brown hue.

Servings: 4

Prepping Time: 15 minutes

Cook Time: 15 minutes

Difficulty: Easy

Ingredients:

- ✓ 8 pre-made biscuit dough
- ✓ 4 large eggs
- ✓ 4 slices of bacon
- ✓ 1 cup shredded cheddar cheese
- ✓ Salt and pepper to taste

Step-by-Step Preparation:

1. Preheat your air fryer to 350°F.

2. Cook bacon slices in the air fryer for 8-10 minutes until crispy. Remove and set aside.

3. Scramble the eggs in a pan, adding salt and pepper to taste. Set aside.

4. Cut each biscuit in half. Layer one half with scrambled eggs, a slice of bacon, and some shredded cheese. Top with the other half of the biscuit.

5. Place the assembled biscuits in the air fryer and cook for 5-7 minutes or until the biscuits are golden-brown and the cheese is melted.

Nutritional Facts: (Per serving)

- ❖ Calories: 520
- ❖ Protein: 20g
- ❖ Carbs: 40g
- ❖ Fat: 30g

These Air Fryer Bacon, Egg, and Cheese Biscuits are a fabulous combination of flavors and textures, promising to liven up your breakfast routine. The air fryer gives a remarkable crispness to the bacon and a beautiful golden color to the biscuits. These are incredibly satisfying, easy to make, and a hit with the whole family. Enjoy a wholesome, delicious breakfast!

Recipe 80: Protein Power Smoothie Bowl

Kickstart your day with the Air Fryer Protein Power Smoothie Bowl, loaded with goodness. This heart-healthy, vegan-friendly meal provides a rich protein source while tantalizing your taste buds with its delightful flavors.

Servings: 2

Prepping Time: 10 minutes

Cook Time: 15 minutes

Difficulty: Easy

Ingredients:

- ✓ 2 ripe bananas
- ✓ 1 cup mixed berries
- ✓ 2 scoops of vegan protein powder
- ✓ 1 cup almond milk
- ✓ 1 tbsp chia seeds
- ✓ 1 tbsp flax seeds

- ✓ 2 tbsp granola
- ✓ Fresh fruits for topping

Step-by-Step Preparation:

1. Preheat your air fryer to 180°C.
2. Combine bananas, mixed berries, protein powder, and almond milk in a blender. Blend until smooth.
3. Pour the smoothie into two heat-safe bowls and sprinkle chia seeds, flax seeds, and granola on top.
4. Carefully place the bowls in the air fryer and cook for about 15 minutes until the top is crispy.
5. Remove from the air fryer, let cool slightly, then top with your favorite fresh fruits before serving.

Nutritional Facts: (Per serving)

- ❖ Calories: 350
- ❖ Protein: 20g
- ❖ Fat: 9g
- ❖ Carbohydrates: 50g
- ❖ Fiber: 10g
- ❖ Sugar: 20g

This Air Fryer Protein Power Smoothie Bowl is ideal for a nutritious, delicious breakfast or a post-workout snack. It's a tasty way to fuel your body while delighting your palate.

Chapter 9: High Protein Desserts

Recipe 81: Air Fryer Protein Brownies

Give your sweet tooth a healthful twist with these Air Fryer Protein Brownies. Rich, fudgy, and protein-packed, they're the perfect post-workout snack or guilt-free dessert to satiate your chocolate cravings.

Servings: 6

Prepping Time: 10 minutes

Cook Time: 15 minutes

Difficulty: Easy

Ingredients:

- ✓ 1 cup chocolate protein powder
- ✓ 1/2 cup almond flour
- ✓ 1/2 cup unsweetened cocoa powder
- ✓ 1/2 cup unsweetened applesauce

- ✓ 2 eggs
- ✓ 1/4 cup almond milk
- ✓ 1 tsp vanilla extract

Step-by-Step Preparation:

1. Combine protein powder, almond flour, and cocoa powder in a bowl.
2. Beat in eggs, then add applesauce, almond milk, and vanilla extract. Mix until smooth.
3. Spoon the batter into an air fryer-safe pan.
4. Air fry at 320°F for 15 minutes or until a toothpick comes out clean.
5. Allow to cool before slicing and serving.

Nutritional Facts: (Per serving)

- ❖ Calories: 220
- ❖ Protein: 20g
- ❖ Carbs: 15g
- ❖ Fat: 8g
- ❖ Fiber: 5g
- ❖ Sugar: 5g

These Air Fryer Protein Brownies are more than a dessert; they're a delightful blend of indulgence and nutrition. Enjoy these post-workouts, a guilt-free treat any time of the day, knowing they're as beneficial to your health as they are pleasing to your palate.

Recipe 82: Protein-Packed Apple Fritters

Packed with protein and natural sweetness, our Air Fryer Protein Packed Apple Fritters are the perfect start or end to your day. Enjoy these guilt-free treats that are as nutritious as they are delicious and perfectly crispy without deep-frying!

Servings: 4

Prepping Time: 10 minutes

Cook Time: 15 minutes

Difficulty: Easy

Ingredients:

- ✓ 2 large apples (cored and diced)
- ✓ 1 cup protein powder
- ✓ 1/2 cup almond flour
- ✓ 1/4 cup honey
- ✓ 1 teaspoon cinnamon
- ✓ 1/2 teaspoon baking powder

- ✓ 1/4 teaspoon salt
- ✓ 2 eggs
- ✓ Cooking spray

Step-by-Step Preparation:

1. In a bowl, combine apples, protein powder, almond flour, honey, cinnamon, baking powder, salt, and eggs. Mix until well combined.
2. Preheat your air fryer to 350°F (175°C).
3. Form the mixture into small fritter shapes and place them into the air fryer basket, ensuring they are not touching.
4. Spray lightly with cooking spray.
5. Cook for 15 minutes or until golden brown and crispy.
6. Let cool before serving. Enjoy!

Nutritional Facts: (Per serving)

- ❖ Calories: 260
- ❖ Fat: 12g
- ❖ Carbohydrates: 22g
- ❖ Sugar: 12g
- ❖ Fiber: 5g
- ❖ Protein: 20g

These protein-packed apple fritters are a must-try for health-conscious individuals with sweet teeth. They're not just good for you; they're delicious, too, balancing sweetness and nutrition perfectly. Experience the joy of indulging without guilt with these air-fried treats today. Say goodbye to unhealthy snacking, and hello to your new favorite recipe!

Recipe 83: Banana Nut Protein Muffins

Welcome to your new favorite breakfast or snack: Air Fryer Banana Nut Protein Muffins! These moist, delicious muffins are perfect for a nutritious on-the-go or post-workout snack.

Servings: 12 muffins

Prepping Time: 15 minutes

Cook Time: 15 minutes

Difficulty: Easy

Ingredients:

- ✓ 2 ripe bananas
- ✓ 1/2 cup of chopped nuts (walnuts or pecans)
- ✓ 2 eggs
- ✓ 1/2 cup of protein powder (vanilla or unflavored)
- ✓ 1/2 cup of almond flour
- ✓ 1/4 cup of honey

- ✓ 1 teaspoon of baking powder
- ✓ 1/2 teaspoon of vanilla extract

Step-by-Step Preparation:

1. In a large bowl, mash the ripe bananas.
2. Add the eggs, honey, and vanilla extract to the bowl and mix until well combined.
3. Stir in the protein powder, almond flour, and baking powder.
4. Fold in the chopped nuts.
5. Spoon the batter into a greased muffin tin that fits your air fryer.
6. Set the air fryer to 350°F and bake for 15 minutes, or until a toothpick comes out clean.
7. Let the muffins cool before removing them from the tin.

Nutritional Facts: (Per muffin)

- ❖ Calories: 140
- ❖ Protein: 7g
- ❖ Carbohydrates: 15g
- ❖ Fat: 6g
- ❖ Fiber: 2g
- ❖ Sugar: 9g

The Air Fryer Banana Nut Protein Muffins are as delightful to eat as they make. Snacks are a quick and nourishing treat. Enjoy the goodness of bananas and nuts in every bite!

Recipe 84: Greek Yogurt Cheesecake Bites

Welcome to a healthy and delicious journey. Air Fryer Greek Yogurt Cheesecake Bites are tiny delights perfect for satisfying your sweet tooth without breaking your diet. They're a protein-packed dessert made with Greek yogurt and a nutty crust that's as nourishing as indulgent. These bites are a delight that'll make every health-conscious dessert lover rejoice!

Servings: 15 pieces

Prepping Time: 10 minutes

Cook Time: 20 minutes

Difficulty: Easy

Ingredients:

- ✓ 2 cups of Greek yogurt
- ✓ 1/2 cup of honey
- ✓ 1 tablespoon of vanilla extract
- ✓ 1 cup of almond flour
- ✓ 2 tablespoons of melted unsalted butter

- ✓ 2 eggs
- ✓ Zest one lemon
- ✓ 1/4 teaspoon of sea salt

Step-by-Step Preparation:

1. Combine almond flour and melted butter in a mixing bowl to form the crust. Press this mixture into a silicone mold suitable for your air fryer.
2. Mix Greek yogurt, honey, vanilla extract, eggs, and lemon zest in another bowl until well combined. Pour this mixture over the crust in the silicone mold.
3. Air fry at 320°F for 20 minutes or until the bites are firm and lightly golden.
4. Allow to cool before removing from the mold. Chill in the fridge before serving.

Nutritional Facts (per serving):

- ❖ Calories: 120
- ❖ Protein: 5g
- ❖ Carbohydrates: 10g
- ❖ Fat: 7g
- ❖ Sugar: 8g
- ❖ Fiber: 1g

Now, isn't that a fantastic twist on a traditional treat? These Air Fryer Greek Yogurt Cheesecake Bites are palatable, simple to prepare, healthy, and ideal for snacking or entertaining. Packed with the goodness of Greek yogurt, they're a dessert that can be guilt-free. Dive into this innovative culinary creation and experience a new dimension of healthy and tasty desserts!

Recipe 85: Almond Joy Protein Balls

Enjoy these easy-to-make, delicious Air Fryer Almond Joy Protein Balls. With a perfect balance of nutrients, they make an ideal post-workout snack or guilt-free dessert, satisfying your sweet tooth and promoting muscle recovery simultaneously.

Servings: 10

Prepping Time: 15 minutes

Cook Time: 10 minutes

Difficulty: Easy

Ingredients:

- 1 cup almond flour
- 1 scoop of chocolate protein powder
- 2 tablespoons raw honey
- 1/4 cup unsweetened shredded coconut
- 1/4 cup chopped almonds
- 1/4 cup mini dark chocolate chips

- ✓ 2 tablespoons almond butter

Step-by-Step Preparation:

1. In a bowl, combine the almond flour, protein powder, honey, and almond butter until well combined.
2. Stir in the shredded coconut, chopped almonds, and chocolate chips.
3. Form them into small balls and place them on the air fryer tray.
4. Air fry at 350°F for 10 minutes or until slightly golden.
5. Allow to cool before enjoying.

Nutritional Facts: (Per serving)

- ❖ Calories: 190
- ❖ Fat: 10g
- ❖ Carbohydrates: 15g
- ❖ Fiber: 3g
- ❖ Protein: 10g

These Air Fryer Almond Joy Protein Balls are nutritious snacks that are as delicious as beneficial. Pack them for on-the-go energy, enjoy them after a workout, or indulge in a dessert that won't derail your healthy eating goals.

Recipe 86: Pumpkin Protein Donuts

Embrace the festive season with our Air Fryer Pumpkin Protein Donuts. These delicious, guilt-free treats perfectly blend the fall flavors of pumpkin and spices with a protein punch. It's your perfect workout buddy and a delightful snack.

Servings: 8

Prepping Time: 15 minutes

Cook Time: 15 minutes

Difficulty: Easy

Ingredients:

- ✓ 1 cup canned pumpkin puree
- ✓ 2 eggs
- ✓ 1/4 cup honey
- ✓ 1 cup protein powder
- ✓ 1 tsp baking powder
- ✓ 1/2 tsp cinnamon

- ✓ 1/4 tsp nutmeg
- ✓ 1/4 tsp salt
- ✓ Sugar-free icing and pumpkin seeds for garnish (optional)

Step-by-Step Preparation:

1. Combine pumpkin puree, eggs, and honey in a bowl.
2. Mix the protein powder, baking powder, cinnamon, nutmeg, and salt in another bowl.
3. Gradually mix dry ingredients into the wet until well combined.
4. Pour batter into a donut mold, filling each cavity 3/4 full.
5. Cook in the air fryer at 350°F for 15 minutes.
6. Allow to cool, then garnish with sugar-free icing and pumpkin seeds, if desired.

Nutritional Facts: (Per donut)

- ❖ Calories: 110
- ❖ Protein: 10g
- ❖ Carbs: 14g
- ❖ Fat: 3g
- ❖ Fiber: 2g

Treat yourself to these delicious Air Fryer Pumpkin Protein Donuts. They're deliciously satisfying and packed with proteins, making them a fantastic post-workout snack or a festive treat. Get creative with your toppings, enjoy, and share this healthy donut recipe!

Recipe 87: High Protein Lemon Bars

Enjoy these guilt-free, high-protein lemon bars. Crafted with a wholegrain base and zesty lemon filling, they perfectly balance tart and sweet. Made in an air fryer, they are a health-conscious delight that tastes heavenly.

Servings: 16 bars

Prepping Time: 20 minutes

Cook Time: 20 minutes

Difficulty: Easy

Ingredients:

- ✓ 1 1/2 cups wholegrain flour
- ✓ 1/2 cup vanilla protein powder
- ✓ 1/2 cup unsweetened applesauce
- ✓ 1/4 cup honey
- ✓ 1 tsp baking powder
- ✓ 4 large lemons (zest and juice)

- ✓ 4 eggs
- ✓ 1/2 cup granulated sweetener (stevia or erythritol)

Step-by-Step Preparation:

1. Preheat your air fryer to 350°F.
2. Mix the flour, protein powder, applesauce, honey, and baking powder to form the base. Press this mixture into a greased baking dish that fits into your air fryer.
3. Whisk the eggs, sweetener, lemon juice, and zest in another bowl. Pour this mixture over the base.
4. Air fry for about 20 minutes or until the filling is set.
5. Allow to cool before cutting into bars.

Nutritional Facts: (Per serving)

- ❖ Calories: 130
- ❖ Protein: 7g
- ❖ Carbohydrates: 18g
- ❖ Fats: 3g
- ❖ Fiber: 2g
- ❖ Sugar: 8g

These air fryer high-protein lemon bars redefine dessert. Tangy, sweet, and surprisingly nutritious, they make a great post-workout snack or guilt-free indulgence. You'll love the ease of the air fryer and the freshness of these delicious lemon bars.

Recipe 88: Peanut Butter Protein Cookies

Enjoy a batch of guilt-free Air Fryer Peanut Butter Protein Cookies. These cookies are perfect for a post-workout treat or a healthy mid-afternoon snack.

Servings: 12 cookies

Prepping Time: 10 minutes

Cook Time: 12 minutes

Difficulty: Easy

Ingredients:

- ✓ 1 cup creamy natural peanut butter
- ✓ 1/2 cup honey
- ✓ 1 egg
- ✓ 1/2 cup vanilla protein powder
- ✓ 1/2 tsp baking soda
- ✓ Chocolate chips (optional)

Step-by-Step Preparation:

1. Mix peanut butter, honey, and egg until smooth in a bowl.
2. Stir in protein powder and baking soda.
3. Roll dough into 12 balls and flatten with a fork, making a crisscross pattern.
4. Preheat your air fryer to 350°F (175°C).
5. Bake in the air fryer for 10-12 minutes or until golden brown.
6. Let the cookies cool for a few minutes before enjoying them.

Nutritional Facts: (per cookie)

- Calories: 180
- Protein: 9g
- Carbs: 16g
- Fat: 10g
- Fiber: 2g

This easy-to-make, delicious, and nutritious recipe for Air Fryer Peanut Butter Protein Cookies is a testament to the versatility of the air fryer. Whether you're a fitness enthusiast looking for a protein-rich snack or just a cookie lover searching for healthier options, these cookies will satisfy your cravings.

Recipe 89: Strawberry Protein Crepes

Delight in a healthy yet indulgent treat with our Air Fryer Strawberry Protein Crepes recipe. This meal combines the sweetness of strawberries with the protein boost of your favorite powder, all wrapped in a light, airy crepe. Enjoy a satisfying breakfast or a guilt-free dessert with this recipe.

Servings: 4

Prepping Time: 15 minutes

Cook Time: 20 minutes

Difficulty: Easy

Ingredients:

- ✓ 1 cup of all-purpose flour
- ✓ 2 eggs
- ✓ 1/2 cup of low-fat milk
- ✓ 1 scoop of protein powder (vanilla or unflavored)
- ✓ 1 tablespoon of melted unsalted butter
- ✓ 1/4 teaspoon of salt

- ✓ 1 cup of fresh strawberries (hulled and sliced)
- ✓ 2 tablespoons of honey

Step-by-Step Preparation:

1. In a bowl, whisk together flour, protein powder, and salt.
2. In another bowl, beat the eggs, then add milk and melted butter.
3. Gradually mix the wet ingredients into the dry ones until smooth.
4. Preheat the air fryer to 375°F. Pour a quarter of the batter into a non-stick crepe pan, ensuring it spreads evenly.
5. Cook each crepe in the air fryer for 5 minutes, then flip and cook for 3 minutes.
6. Repeat the process with the remaining batter.
7. Fill each crepe with strawberries, drizzle with honey, fold, and serve.

Nutritional Facts: (Per serving)

- ❖ Calories: 245
- ❖ Protein: 13g
- ❖ Fat: 6g
- ❖ Carbs: 34g
- ❖ Fiber: 2g
- ❖ Sugar: 12g

These Air Fryer Strawberry Protein Crepes offer a delightful blend of taste and nutrition. The crepes are fluffy and light, while the strawberries add a fresh, juicy sweetness. This meal is perfect for kickstarting your day or as a delightful post-workout snack. Enjoy it with a cup of coffee or a refreshing fruit smoothie!

Recipe 90: Chocolate Chip Protein Scones

Kickstart your day with these delightful Air Fryer Chocolate Chip Protein Scones! They're not just tasty but also pack a punch of protein, making them perfect for a nutritious breakfast or a quick snack. Your air fryer does the baking, ensuring a crispy outside and tender inside.

Servings: 8 Scones

Prepping Time: 15 minutes

Cook Time: 15 minutes

Difficulty: Easy

Ingredients:

- 2 cups whole wheat flour
- 1 scoop protein powder (vanilla or unflavored)
- 1/4 cup granulated sugar
- 1 tbsp baking powder
- 1/2 tsp salt
- 1/2 cup unsalted butter, cold and cubed

- ✓ 1/2 cup milk
- ✓ 1 egg
- ✓ 1 tsp vanilla extract
- ✓ 1/2 cup chocolate chips

Step-by-Step Preparation:

1. Combine flour, protein powder, sugar, baking powder, and salt in a bowl.
2. Add the cold butter and use your hands to break it into the mixture until it resembles coarse crumbs.
3. In another bowl, whisk together milk, egg, and vanilla extract.
4. Gradually add the wet ingredients to the dry ones, stirring until combined.
5. Fold in the chocolate chips.
6. Cut the dough into a disk into 8 wedges.
7. Place the scones in the air fryer basket, ensuring they don't overlap.
8. Cook at 350°F for about 15 minutes or until golden brown.
9. Allow them to cool before serving.

Nutritional Facts: (Per serving)

- ❖ Calories: 275 kcal
- ❖ Protein: 8g
- ❖ Fat: 15g
- ❖ Carbohydrates: 30g
- ❖ Fiber: 4g
- ❖ Sugar: 12g

Delight in the perfect blend of health and indulgence with these Air Fryer Chocolate Chip Protein Scones. They're simple to prepare, wholesome, and delicious, making them ideal for morning coffee or afternoon tea. Enjoy your air fryer baked goodies and savor every nutritious bite!

Chapter 10: Full Meal Preps

Recipe 91: Air Fryer BBQ Chicken with Quinoa and Broccoli

Indulge in a nutritious meal with our Air Fryer BBQ Chicken with Quinoa and Broccoli. This balanced dish combines the smoky flavor of BBQ chicken with wholesome quinoa and nutrient-packed broccoli.

Servings: 4

Preparation Time: 15 minutes

Cooking Time: 25 minutes

Difficulty: Easy

Ingredients:

- ✓ 4 boneless, skinless chicken breasts
- ✓ 1 cup BBQ sauce
- ✓ 2 cups quinoa

- ✓ 4 cups water
- ✓ 2 heads of broccoli
- ✓ Salt and pepper to taste
- ✓ Olive oil

Step-by-Step Preparation:

1. Preheat your air fryer to 370°F.
2. Coat the chicken breasts evenly with BBQ sauce and air fry for 20 minutes.
3. While the chicken is cooking, rinse the quinoa under cold water, then cook in a pot with the 4 cups of water until fluffy, about 15 minutes.
4. Cut broccoli into florets, toss with olive oil, salt, and pepper, and roast in the air fryer for 5 minutes.
5. Serve the BBQ chicken on a bed of quinoa and roasted broccoli.

Nutritional Facts: (Per serving)

- ❖ Calories: 650
- ❖ Fat: 12g
- ❖ Protein: 50g
- ❖ Carbohydrates: 85g
- ❖ Fiber: 8g
- ❖ Sugar: 20g

This Air Fryer BBQ Chicken with Quinoa and Broccoli is a well-rounded meal, perfect for a busy weekday or a casual dinner. It's a delicious combination of hearty flavors and wholesome nutrition that your family will love. Bon Appétit!

Recipe 92: Mediterranean Salmon with Couscous and Asparagus

Savour a wholesome and delectable dinner with our Air Fryer Mediterranean Salmon recipe. Succulent salmon and tender asparagus pair perfectly with fluffy couscous, all tossed in a medley of Mediterranean flavors for a light and satisfying meal.

Servings: 4

Prepping Time: 15 minutes

Cook Time: 15 minutes

Difficulty: Easy

Ingredients:

- ✓ 4 salmon fillets
- ✓ 1 bunch of asparagus, trimmed
- ✓ 1 cup couscous
- ✓ 2 cups of water
- ✓ 1 lemon, zested and juiced

- ✓ 4 tablespoons olive oil
- ✓ 2 cloves garlic, minced
- ✓ Salt and pepper to taste
- ✓ 1 teaspoon dried oregano

Step-by-Step Preparation:

1. Preheat the air fryer to 400°F (200°C).
2. Season salmon with lemon zest, garlic, oregano, olive oil, salt, and pepper.
3. Place salmon in the air fryer and cook for 12-15 minutes or until cooked.
4. Meanwhile, cook the couscous as per package instructions.
5. In a pan, sauté the asparagus in the remaining olive oil until tender.
6. Drizzle cooked salmon and asparagus with fresh lemon juice.
7. Serve the salmon and asparagus on a bed of couscous.

Nutritional Facts: (Per serving)

- ❖ Calories: 487 kcal
- ❖ Fat: 19g
- ❖ Saturated Fat: 3g
- ❖ Protein: 40g
- ❖ Carbohydrates: 40g
- ❖ Fiber: 4g
- ❖ Sugar: 3g
- ❖ Sodium: 101mg

Delight in this Air Fryer Mediterranean Salmon that marries the rich flavors of the sea with the wholesome goodness of veggies and grains. Easy to prepare and wonderfully balanced, it's an ideal dish to inspire your weeknight dinners or to impress on a special occasion.

Recipe 93: Beef and Broccoli Stir Fry

Dive into the enticing blend of flavors this Air Fryer Beef and Broccoli Stir Fry offer. A healthier take on the classic Chinese dish brings together tender beef and crunchy broccoli with a delightful sauce. All made easy with your air fryer.

Servings: 4

Prep Time: 15 minutes

Cook Time: 15 minutes

Difficulty: Easy

Ingredients:

- ✓ 1 lb beef sirloin, thinly sliced
- ✓ 2 cups broccoli florets
- ✓ 2 tablespoons soy sauce
- ✓ 1 tablespoon oyster sauce
- ✓ 1 tablespoon sesame oil
- ✓ 2 cloves garlic, minced

- ✓ 1 tablespoon cornstarch
- ✓ Salt and pepper to taste

Step-by-Step Preparation:

1. Preheat the air fryer to 400°F (200°C).
2. Marinate beef with soy sauce, oyster sauce, sesame oil, garlic, cornstarch, salt, and pepper in a bowl. Let it rest for 10 minutes.
3. Place the marinated beef in the air fryer basket, and cook for 10 minutes.
4. Add the broccoli florets and cook for an additional 5 minutes.
5. Stir to combine and ensure the broccoli is coated in the sauce.

Nutritional Facts: (Per serving)

- ❖ Calories: 295
- ❖ Protein: 28g
- ❖ Carbohydrates: 9g
- ❖ Fat: 16g
- ❖ Fiber: 2g
- ❖ Sugar: 2g

This quick and easy Air Fryer Beef and Broccoli Stir Fry will make your taste buds dance with its savory flavors. The best part? It's low in carbs and protein, making it perfect for a healthy weeknight meal. Why not give this simple yet tasty recipe a try tonight?

Recipe 94: Grilled Turkey with Sweet Potatoes and Brussels Sprouts

Experience the magic of holiday flavors any day of the year with Air Fryer Grilled Turkey, served with nutrient-rich Sweet Potatoes and Brussels Sprouts. This quick, healthy recipe combines the juiciness of turkey with the subtle sweetness of the vegetables, creating a dinner sensation everyone will love.

Servings: 4

Prepping Time: 20 minutes

Cook Time: 45 minutes

Difficulty: Intermediate

Ingredients:

- ✓ 1kg Turkey breast
- ✓ 4 Sweet Potatoes, cubed
- ✓ 500g Brussels Sprouts, halved
- ✓ 3 tbsp Olive oil

- ✓ Salt and Pepper to taste
- ✓ 1 tsp Garlic powder
- ✓ 1 tsp Rosemary, dried
- ✓ 1/2 Lemon, juiced

Step-by-Step Preparation:

1. Preheat your air fryer to 180°C (350°F).
2. Rub the turkey breast with half the olive oil, lemon juice, garlic powder, Rosemary, salt, and Pepper.
3. Place the turkey in the air fryer for 30 minutes.
4. Toss sweet potatoes and Brussels sprouts with olive oil, salt, and Pepper in a bowl.
5. After 30 minutes, add the vegetables to the air fryer and cook for another 15 minutes until the turkey is fully cooked and the vegetables are tender.
6. Let it rest for a few minutes before slicing the turkey.

Nutritional Facts: (Per Serving)

- ❖ Calories: 550
- ❖ Protein: 60g
- ❖ Fat: 15g
- ❖ Carbohydrates: 45g
- ❖ Fiber: 10g
- ❖ Sodium: 250mg

This delightful Air Fryer Grilled Turkey with Sweet Potatoes and Brussels Sprouts recipe delivers a beautiful blend of textures and flavors. It's a feast for the taste buds and a visual treat. With health benefits, this dish will quickly become a staple in your cooking repertoire. Enjoy a wholesome meal with your loved ones without sacrificing taste or quality.

Recipe 95: Lemon Garlic Shrimp with Zucchini Noodles

Savor the freshness of summer with this delightful Air Fryer Lemon Garlic Shrimp paired with Zucchini Noodles. Low-carb and full of flavor, it's a breeze to prepare and perfect for a healthy weeknight meal.

Servings: 4

Prepping Time: 15 minutes

Cook Time: 10 minutes

Difficulty: Easy

Ingredients:

- ✓ 1 lb of large shrimp, peeled and deveined
- ✓ 1 tablespoon olive oil
- ✓ 2 cloves of garlic, minced
- ✓ Zest and juice of one lemon
- ✓ Salt and pepper to taste

- ✓ 4 medium zucchini, spiralized
- ✓ 2 tablespoons of fresh parsley, chopped

Step-by-Step Preparation:

1. Preheat your air fryer to 400 degrees F (200 degrees C).
2. Combine the shrimp, olive oil, garlic, lemon zest, and juice in a bowl. Season with salt and pepper.
3. Place the shrimp mixture in the air fryer and cook for 5-7 minutes or until shrimp are pink and cooked through.
4. While the shrimp are cooking, spiralize the zucchini and sauté in a pan with some olive oil until tender.
5. Once done, mix the cooked shrimp and zucchini noodles.
6. Garnish with fresh parsley before serving.

Nutritional Facts: (Per Serving)

- ❖ Calories: 220 kcal
- ❖ Protein: 24 g
- ❖ Fat: 7 g
- ❖ Carbohydrates: 16 g
- ❖ Fiber: 3 g
- ❖ Sugar: 6 g

This Air Fryer Lemon Garlic Shrimp with Zucchini Noodles will satisfy you with its simplicity and a burst of flavors. It's an excellent dish for those seeking a healthy, light meal without compromising taste. Enjoy!

Recipe 96: Asian Inspired Chicken and Vegetable Stir Fry

Savor the exotic flavors of Asia with this delightful Air Fryer Asian-Inspired Chicken and Vegetable Stir Fry. It's a harmonious blend of colorful veggies, tender chicken, and a savory-sweet sauce, all cooked perfectly in an air fryer.

Servings: 4

Prepping Time: 20 minutes

Cook Time: 20 minutes

Difficulty: Medium

Ingredients:

- ✓ 2 boneless, skinless chicken breasts
- ✓ 1 bell pepper, sliced
- ✓ 1 carrot, sliced
- ✓ 1 onion, chopped
- ✓ 2 cloves garlic, minced

- ✓ 2 tablespoons soy sauce
- ✓ 1 tablespoon hoisin sauce
- ✓ 1 tablespoon sesame oil
- ✓ Salt and pepper to taste
- ✓ Sesame seeds and chopped green onions for garnish

Step-by-Step Preparation:

1. Preheat the air fryer to 360°F.
2. Season chicken with salt and pepper, then air fry for 12 minutes until cooked. Remove and set aside.
3. In the same fryer, air fry the vegetables for 8 minutes until they are tender-crisp.
4. Mix soy sauce, hoisin sauce, and sesame oil in a small bowl.
5. Add the cooked chicken and sauce to the vegetables in the air fryer. Stir well and air fry for an additional 3 minutes.
6. Garnish with sesame seeds and chopped green onions before serving.

Nutritional Facts: (Per Serving)

- ❖ Calories: 210
- ❖ Fat: 7g
- ❖ Carbohydrates: 12g
- ❖ Protein: 24g
- ❖ Fiber: 3g
- ❖ Sodium: 550mg

This Air Fryer Asian-Inspired Chicken and Vegetable Stir Fry is a quick, healthy, and flavorful meal that brings the zest of Asia to your table. With a crisp texture and a rich, savory sauce, this recipe will surely be a hit at your next dinner gathering.

Recipe 97: Pork Tenderloin with Sweet Potatoes and Green Beans

Elevate your dinner with this Air Fryer Pork Tenderloin recipe, accompanied by delicious sweet potatoes and green beans. This savory and balanced meal is easy to prepare and brimming with flavors, perfect for a midweek feast or a special occasion.

Servings: 4

Prepping Time: 15 minutes

Cook Time: 25 minutes

Difficulty: Easy

Ingredients:

- ✓ 1 Pork Tenderloin (1lb)
- ✓ 2 Sweet Potatoes, diced
- ✓ 2 cups Green Beans, trimmed
- ✓ 2 tablespoons Olive Oil
- ✓ Salt and Pepper to taste

- ✓ 1 tablespoon Paprika
- ✓ 1 tablespoon Garlic Powder
- ✓ 1 tablespoon Onion Powder

Step-by-Step Preparation:

1. Preheat your air fryer to 400°F (200°C).
2. Season the pork tenderloin with salt, Pepper, paprika, garlic powder, and onion powder.
3. Place the tenderloin in the air fryer basket and cook for 10 minutes.
4. Toss the sweet potatoes and green beans in olive oil, salt, and Pepper.
5. Add the veggies to the air fryer basket and cook for 15 minutes until the pork and the vegetables are tender.
6. Let the pork rest for a few minutes before slicing.

Nutritional Facts: (Per Serving)

- ❖ Calories: 295
- ❖ Total Fat: 10g
- ❖ Saturated Fat: 2g
- ❖ Cholesterol: 85mg
- ❖ Sodium: 250mg
- ❖ Total Carbohydrates: 20g
- ❖ Dietary Fiber: 5g
- ❖ Sugars: 5g
- ❖ Protein: 30g

This Air Fryer Pork Tenderloin with Sweet Potatoes and Green Beans offers a beautiful medley of flavors. It's healthy, easy to prepare, and satisfying. The succulent pork paired with hearty veggies makes a dish as visually appealing as it is tasty. Savor and enjoy the culinary delight that awaits you.

Recipe 98: Cajun Catfish with Rice and Okra

Enjoy a taste of the South with this Air Fryer Cajun Catfish with Rice and Okra recipe. This dish boasts bold, spicy flavors, crispy air-fried catfish, creamy rice, and succulent okra that will impress your dinner guests and family.

Servings: 4

Prepping Time: 20 minutes

Cook Time: 20 minutes

Difficulty: Intermediate

Ingredients:

- 4 catfish fillets
- 2 tablespoons Cajun seasoning
- 1 cup long-grain rice
- 2 cups fresh okra, sliced
- 1 tablespoon olive oil
- Salt and pepper to taste

- ✓ 2 cups chicken stock
- ✓ Lemon wedges for garnish

Step-by-Step Preparation:

1. Preheat your air fryer to 400°F (200°C).
2. Season the catfish fillets with Cajun seasoning, salt, and pepper.
3. Cook the rice in chicken stock until tender, then set aside and keep warm.
4. Toss the okra in olive oil, then season with salt and pepper.
5. Air fry the catfish fillets for 10 minutes, flipping halfway.
6. Also, air fry the okra for 10 minutes, stirring occasionally.
7. Serve the crispy catfish over the creamy rice, topped with the fried okra. Garnish with a wedge of lemon.

Nutritional Facts: (Per Serving)

- ❖ Calories: 450
- ❖ Protein: 34g
- ❖ Fat: 15g
- ❖ Carbohydrates: 45g
- ❖ Sodium: 780mg
- ❖ Fiber: 4g

Air Fryer Cajun Catfish with Rice and Okra is the perfect wholesome meal for a cozy night. Full of southern charm, this dish combines the spice of Cajun seasoning with the crunch of air-fried catfish, the creaminess of rice, and the earthy taste of okra for an unforgettable dining experience. Serve with a squeeze of fresh lemon for an added zing.

Recipe 99: Stuffed Bell Peppers with Ground Turkey and Brown Rice

Delight in the hearty and healthy flavors of these Air Fryer Stuffed Bell Peppers with Ground Turkey and Brown Rice. This dish is perfect for a nourishing weeknight dinner or a festive gathering with a rich mix of protein, fiber, and vitamins.

Servings: 4

Prepping Time: 15 Minutes

Cook Time: 25 Minutes

Difficulty: Easy

Ingredients

- ✓ 4 bell peppers, tops removed and seeded
- ✓ 1 pound ground turkey
- ✓ 1 cup cooked brown rice
- ✓ 1 medium onion, diced
- ✓ 2 cloves garlic, minced

- ✓ 1 can (14.5 oz) diced tomatoes, drained
- ✓ 1 tsp chili powder
- ✓ Salt and pepper to taste
- ✓ 1 cup shredded cheddar cheese

Step-by-Step Preparation

1. Preheat the air fryer to 370°F.
2. In a pan, sauté the onion, garlic, and ground turkey until cooked.
3. Add diced tomatoes, cooked brown rice, chili powder, salt, and pepper. Mix well.
4. Fill each bell pepper with the turkey and rice mixture.
5. Place the stuffed peppers in the air fryer for 15 minutes.
6. Sprinkle shredded cheese on top and cook for another 10 minutes or until the cheese is melted and slightly golden.

Nutritional Facts: (Per Serving)

- ❖ Calories: 320
- ❖ Protein: 20g
- ❖ Carbohydrates: 30g
- ❖ Fat: 12g
- ❖ Fiber: 5g
- ❖ Sodium: 720mg
- ❖ Sugars: 4g

These Air Fryer Stuffed Bell Peppers with Ground Turkey and Brown Rice are delicious and nutritious. They are a great low-calorie option that doesn't compromise taste or satisfaction. Enjoy this meal that will be a crowd-pleaser and a frequent request in your kitchen!

Recipe 100: Spicy Sausage and Vegetable Skillet

Savor the flavor explosion of Air Fryer Spicy Sausage and Vegetable Skillet. It's a quick, low-maintenance meal that packs a hearty punch with delicious spicy sausages, colorful veggies, and savory spices, all cooked to perfection in an air fryer.

Servings: 4

Prepping Time: 10 minutes

Cook Time: 15 minutes

Difficulty: Easy

Ingredients:

- ✓ 4 spicy sausages
- ✓ 1 bell pepper, chopped
- ✓ 1 onion, chopped
- ✓ 2 zucchinis, chopped
- ✓ 1 tablespoon olive oil

- ✓ Salt and pepper to taste
- ✓ 1 teaspoon smoked paprika
- ✓ 1/2 teaspoon cayenne pepper

Step-by-Step Preparation:

1. Preheat the air fryer to 400°F (200°C).
2. Combine the sausages, bell pepper, onion, zucchini, olive oil, and spices in a large bowl. Mix until everything is well-coated.
3. Transfer the mixture to the air fryer basket and cook for 15 minutes, shaking the basket halfway through cooking.
4. Check the sausages for doneness before serving. They should be browned and fully cooked through.

Nutritional Facts: (Per Serving)

- ❖ Calories: 250
- ❖ Fat: 15g
- ❖ Carbohydrates: 10g
- ❖ Protein: 20g

Whether you're cooking for a busy weeknight dinner or a casual weekend brunch, this Air Fryer Spicy Sausage and Vegetable Skillet is a surefire hit. Quick to prepare and packed with nutrition, it's a delightful dish that brings the best of comfort food to your table without the hassle of elaborate cooking.

Recipe 101: Easter Lamb with Rosemary and Garlic

Indulge in a festive feast with this mouthwatering Air Fryer Easter Lamb seasoned with rosemary and garlic. This recipe guarantees a succulent and perfectly cooked lamb, enveloped with a crust rich with the savory scent of herbs and spices.

Servings: 6

Prepping Time: 15 minutes

Cook Time: 90 minutes

Difficulty: Moderate

Ingredients:

- ✓ 1 bone-in leg of lamb (about 2-3 kg)
- ✓ 6 cloves of garlic, minced
- ✓ 4 tablespoons of fresh rosemary, finely chopped
- ✓ 2 tablespoons of olive oil
- ✓ Salt and freshly ground black pepper to taste

Step-by-Step Preparation:

1. Pat the lamb dry and make small incisions over the meat.
2. Mix the garlic, rosemary, olive oil, salt, and pepper in a bowl.
3. Rub this mixture all over the lamb, ensuring it gets into the incisions.
4. Preheat the air fryer to 180°C (350°F).
5. Cook the lamb in the air fryer for about 1.5 hours or until it reaches your desired level of doneness.
6. Let it rest for 10 minutes before carving.

Nutritional Facts: (Per Serving)

- Calories: 250
- Fat: 15g
- Carbohydrates: 10g
- Protein: 20g

Celebrate Easter with this Air Fryer Easter Lamb with Rosemary and Garlic that will tantalize your taste buds. The best part? You can enjoy a deliciously tender lamb roast without spending the whole day in the kitchen. Pair it with your favorite Easter sides, and you're ready to feast!

Conclusion

In conclusion, Ava Mitchell's **"High Protein Air Fryer Recipes Cookbook with Picture"** is an absolute must-have for both amateur and seasoned cooks. Attention-grabbing with its stunning visuals and creative high-protein recipes, the book makes a compelling case for nutritious cooking in the modern age. It's an engaging read that captures your interest from the first page, offering a clear guide to creating wholesome, high-protein meals using the air fryer.

The book successfully piques Interest with its collection of 101 recipes that are not only delicious but also healthier alternatives. Ava Mitchell's original recipes challenge conventional cooking methods, opening up a new world of culinary possibilities. Every recipe is complemented by breathtaking images that inspire you to explore and experiment in your kitchen.

"High Protein Air Fryer Recipes Cookbook with Picture" effortlessly stirs Desire by showcasing the ease and efficiency of using an air fryer for daily cooking. The simplicity of the recipes, coupled with Mitchell's expert advice, makes you yearn to start your journey with an air fryer if you haven't already.

Finally, the book incites Action by providing insightful tips and tricks to get the most out of your air fryer, ensuring readers are well-equipped for culinary adventures. With a balance of nutritious meals and decadent treats, this cookbook assures you that healthy eating does not have to be tedious or complicated.

In summary, Ava Mitchell's cookbook is a testament to modern, health-conscious cooking and a perfect addition to your kitchen library. So why wait? Step into the world of high-protein air fryer cooking with Ava Mitchell and get cooking!

Printed in Great Britain
by Amazon